NATIONAL GEOGRAPHIC

W9-CSA-666

Road Atlas

UNITED STATES · CANADA · MEXICO

CONTENTS

Published by MapQuest.com, Inc.
in association with National Geographic Maps
and Melcher Media, Inc.

Scenic Drives Pages 10–21

Detailed route descriptions of 36 of America's most memorable highways and byways help you get off the beaten path and journey into landscapes alive with the presence of history and wildlife.

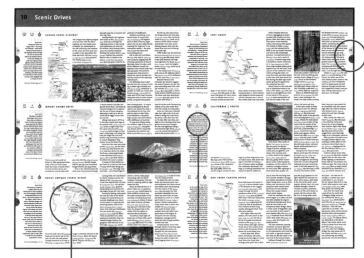

Detailed Route Maps

With specific roadside landmarks spotted, these maps show each drive in detail, aiding point-to-point navigation.

Tips on the Road Ahead

Special "Road Notes" tell you what kind of terrain to expect—for example, mountainous ridges and passes, dense forest, rolling plains, or flat marshland. The notes also give advisories on seasonal road conditions and the advantages of travelling at specific times of year.

Easy Cross-Reference to Road Maps

Each scenic drive features one yellow road map tab for each state or province through which the drive passes. The tabs direct you to the corresponding state road map pages. For example, next to the Lost Coast drive a yellow tab with the number "30" indicates the page on which the California state road maps begin.

Road Maps Pages 22–156

Road maps for all 50 states appear alphabetically, followed by Canadian provinces, organized from west to east. Also included are Mexico and Puerto Rico.

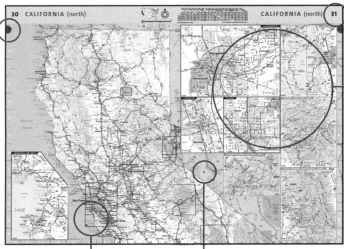

Easy Cross-Reference to Index

On each road map, a red tab indicates the page number for index listings of counties, cities, and towns in that state.

Inset Map Boxes

Red boxes outline areas featured in larger scale. When an inset map does not appear on the same page as its home map, a page number in white type points you to the correct page. For example, the red box with the number "36" above indicates that there is a larger-scale map of the Bay Area on page 36.

Quick Map-to-Map Navigation

Handy yellow buttons indicate adjacent states and their page numbers, making it easier to navigate from state to state. Postal abbreviations are used throughout. For example, "NV" with "88" indicates that the Nevada state road map is on page 88.

Inset Maps

Larger-scale city and downtown maps show the level of detail you need to navigate in a new city. Select national parks and major recreation areas are also highlighted.

Index Pages 156–165

If you need to find your destination on a state map, look it up in this handy index. The index provides page numbers and grid coordinates for cities and counties in each state.

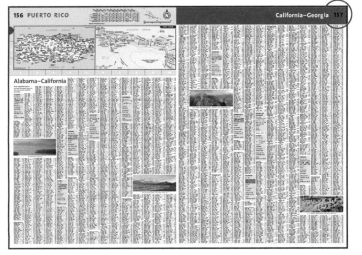

How the Index Works

Listings are alphabetical by state, with cities and towns separate from counties. Canada, Mexico, and Puerto Rico are listed separately. The grid coordinate following each city or town name indicates its location on the state map. Page numbers for the maps are listed in red inside the yellow boxes at the beginning of each state. If a city appears on both a state road map and a metropolitan area map, the grid coordinate will refer to the smaller-scale map. For example, San Francisco is indexed to Northern California on page 30, rather than the Bay Area on page 36.

Road Map Legend

TRANSPORTATION

CONTROLLED ACCESS HIGHWAYS

- Free
- Toll; Toll Booth
- Under Construction
- Interchange and Exit Number
- Ramp
  Downtown maps only
- Rest Area; Service Area
  Yellow with facilities

OTHER HIGHWAYS

- Primary Highway
- Secondary Highway
- Multilane Divided Highway
  Primary and secondary highways only
- Other Paved Road
- Unpaved Road
  Check conditions locally

HIGHWAY MARKERS

- Interstate Route
- U.S. Route
- State or Provincial Route
- County or Other Route
- Business Route
- Trans-Canada Highway
- Canadian Provincial Autoroute
- Mexican Federal Route

OTHER SYMBOLS

- Distances along Major Highways
  Miles in U.S.; kilometers in Canada and Mexico
- Tunnel; Pass
- Driving Tour
  see National Geographic's Driving Guides to America
- Wayside Stop
- One-way Street
- Port of Entry
- Airport
- Railroad
  Downtown maps only
- Auto Ferry; Passenger Ferry

RECREATION AND FEATURES OF INTEREST

- National Park
- National Forest; National Grassland
- Other Large Park or Recreation Area
- Small State Park with and without Camping
- Public Campsite
- Trail
- Point of Interest
- Visitor Information Center
- Public Golf Course; Private Golf Course
  Professional tournament location
- Hospital
  City maps only
- Ski Area

CITIES AND TOWNS

- National Capital; State or Provincial Capital
- County Seat
  State maps only
- Cities, Towns, and Populated Places
  Type size indicates relative importance
- Urban Area
  State and province maps only
- Large Incorporated Cities

OTHER MAP FEATURES

- JEFFERSON — County Boundary and Name
- —40°N 95°W — Latitude; Longitude
- Time Zone Boundary
- Mt. Olympus 7,965 — Mountain Peak; Elevation
  Feet in U.S.; meters in Canada and Mexico
- Perennial; Intermittent River
- Perennial; Intermittent or Dry Water Body
- Dam
- Swamp
- Glacier

TEMPERATURE CONVERSIONS

°F	°C	°C	°F
100	37.8	35	95
90	32.2	30	86
80	26.7	25	77
70	21.1	20	68
60	15.6	15	59
50	10.0	10	50
40	4.4	5	41
32	0	0	32
30	-1.1	-5	23
20	-6.7	-10	14
10	-12.2	-15	5
0	-17.8	-20	-4
-10	-23.3	-25	-13
-20	-28.9	-30	-22
-30	-34.4	-35	-31
-40	-40.0	-40	-40
-50	-45.6	-45	-49

DISTANCE CONVERSIONS

MILES	KM	KM	MILES
1	1.6	1	0.6
5	8.0	2	1.2
10	16.1	5	3.1
15	24.1	10	6.2
20	32.2	15	9.3
25	40.2	20	12.4
30	48.3	25	15.5
35	56.3	30	18.6
40	64.4	40	24.9
45	72.4	50	31.1
50	80.5	60	37.3
55	88.5	70	43.5
60	96.6	80	49.7
65	104.6	90	55.9
70	112.7	100	62.1
75	120.7	110	68.4
80	128.7	120	74.6
85	136.8	130	80.8
90	144.8	140	87.0
95	152.9	150	93.2
100	160.9	160	99.4

VOLUME CONVERSIONS

GALLONS	LITERS	LITERS	GALLONS
1	3.8	1	0.26
2	7.6	2	0.5
3	11.4	3	0.8
4	15.1	4	1.1
5	18.9	5	1.3
10	37.9	10	2.6
15	56.8	20	5.3
20	75.7	30	7.9
25	94.6	40	10.6
30	113.6	50	13.2
40	151.4	75	19.8
50	189.3	100	26.4

Legend:

Interstate Route
Other Route
206 Distance in Miles
4:15 Approximate Travel Time
● Miami City on Mileage Charts, pg. 167-168
● Fort Pierce Other City

Distances and driving times may vary depending on actual route traveled and driving conditions.

© MapQuest.com, Inc.

SUNSHINE

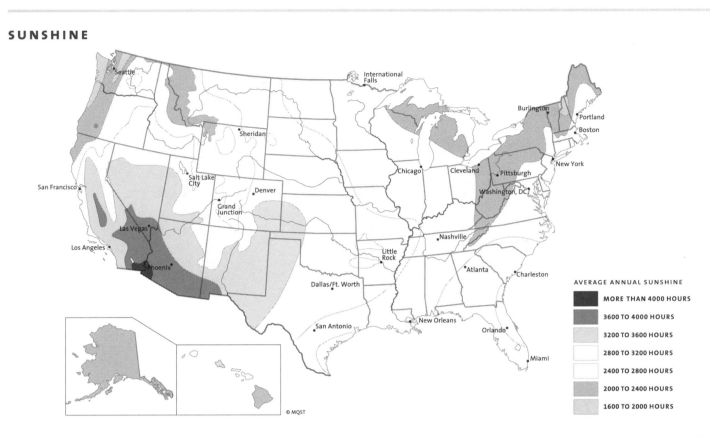

AVERAGE ANNUAL SUNSHINE
- MORE THAN 4000 HOURS
- 3600 TO 4000 HOURS
- 3200 TO 3600 HOURS
- 2800 TO 3200 HOURS
- 2400 TO 2800 HOURS
- 2000 TO 2400 HOURS
- 1600 TO 2000 HOURS

© MQST

CITY	DAYS OF SUNSHINE
Las Vegas, NV	211.1
Phoenix, AZ	211.0
Los Angeles, CA	186.0
San Francisco, CA	160.3
Grand Junction, CO	136.6
Dallas/Fort Worth, TX	135.5
Salt Lake City, UT	125.0
Little Rock, AR	118.7
Denver, CO	115.2
Atlanta, GA	110.4
New York, NY	106.7
San Antonio, TX	106.1
Nashville, TN	102.9
Charleston, SC	102.3
New Orleans, LA	101.4
Portland, ME	101.3
Boston, MA	98.4
Washington, DC	96.7
Sheridan, WY	95.8
Orlando, FL	89.9
Chicago, IL	83.8
International Falls, MN	76.7
Miami, FL	75.1
Seattle, WA	71.0
Cleveland, OH	66.4
Pittsburgh, PA	58.3
Burlington, VT	57.9

RAINFALL

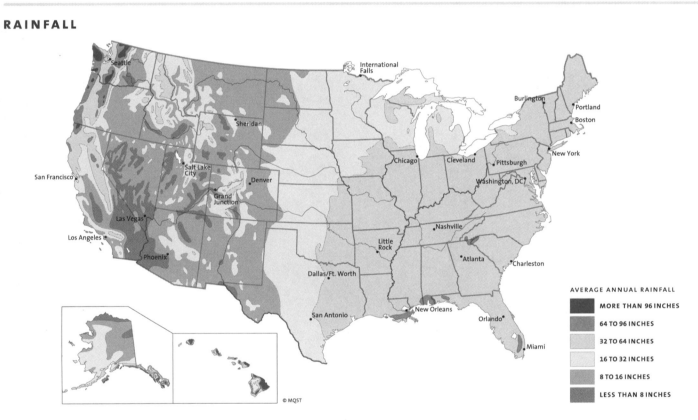

AVERAGE ANNUAL RAINFALL
- MORE THAN 96 INCHES
- 64 TO 96 INCHES
- 32 TO 64 INCHES
- 16 TO 32 INCHES
- 8 TO 16 INCHES
- LESS THAN 8 INCHES

© MQST

CITY	DAYS OF RAINFALL
Cleveland, OH	156.0
Burlington, VT	154.0
Pittsburgh, PA	153.3
Seattle, WA	150.4
International Falls, MN	131.3
Miami, FL	129.5
Portland, ME	128.5
Boston, MA	126.5
Chicago, IL	126.3
New York, NY	120.6
Nashville, TN	118.6
Orlando, FL	115.8
Atlanta, GA	115.1
New Orleans, LA	114.5
Charleston, SC	112.9
Washington, DC	112.3
Sheridan, WY	106.8
Little Rock, AR	104.5
Salt Lake City, UT	90.6
Denver, CO	89.1
San Antonio, TX	82.1
Dallas/Fort Worth, TX	78.9
Grand Junction, CO	72.8
San Francisco, CA	62.0
Phoenix, AZ	36.5
Los Angeles, CA	35.2
Las Vegas, NV	26.5

SNOWFALL

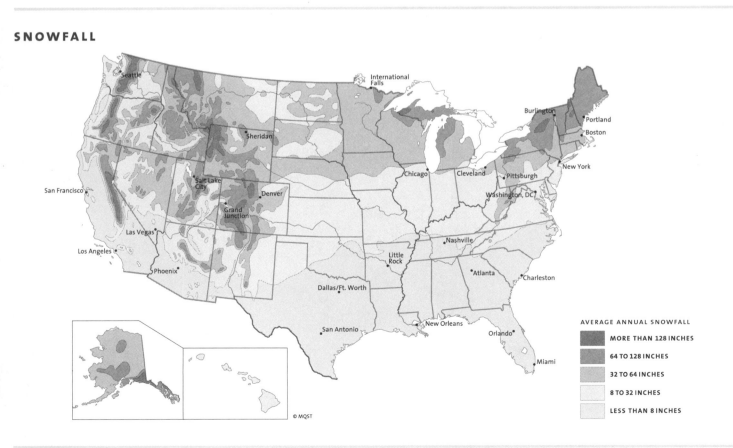

AVERAGE ANNUAL SNOWFALL
- MORE THAN 128 INCHES
- 64 TO 128 INCHES
- 32 TO 64 INCHES
- 8 TO 32 INCHES
- LESS THAN 8 INCHES

© MQST

CITY	DAYS OF SNOWFALL
Sheridan, WY	23.6
Burlington, VT	22.0
International Falls, MN	19.5
Cleveland, OH	18.4
Denver, CO	17.9
Salt Lake City, UT	17.8
Portland, ME	17.3
Pittsburgh, PA	12.8
Chicago, IL	11.6
Boston, MA	10.7
Grand Junction, CO	8.7
New York, NY	7.9
Washington, DC	4.6
Nashville, TN	3.5
Seattle, WA	2.4
Little Rock, AR	1.9
Dallas/Fort Worth, TX	1.1
Atlanta, GA	0.6
Las Vegas, NV	0.4
Charleston, SC	0.2
San Antonio, TX	0.2
New Orleans, LA	rare
San Francisco, CA	rare
Los Angeles, CA	0.0
Miami, FL	0.0
Orlando, FL	0.0
Phoenix, AZ	0.0

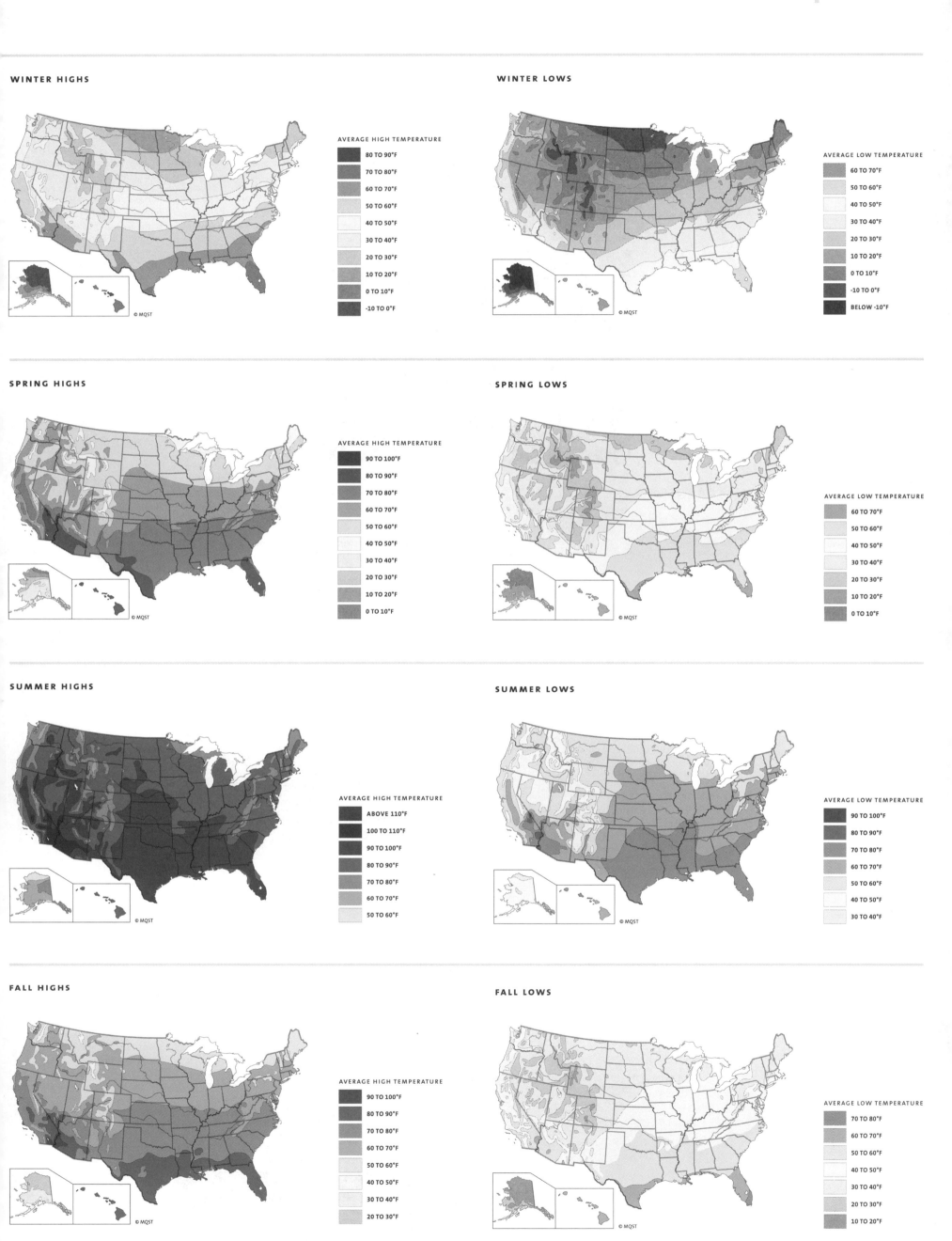

WINTER HIGHS

AVERAGE HIGH TEMPERATURE

80 TO 90°F
70 TO 80°F
60 TO 70°F
50 TO 60°F
40 TO 50°F
30 TO 40°F
20 TO 30°F
10 TO 20°F
0 TO 10°F
-10 TO 0°F

© MQST

WINTER LOWS

AVERAGE LOW TEMPERATURE

60 TO 70°F
50 TO 60°F
40 TO 50°F
30 TO 40°F
20 TO 30°F
10 TO 20°F
0 TO 10°F
-10 TO 0°F
BELOW -10°F

© MQST

SPRING HIGHS

AVERAGE HIGH TEMPERATURE

90 TO 100°F
80 TO 90°F
70 TO 80°F
60 TO 70°F
50 TO 60°F
40 TO 50°F
30 TO 40°F
20 TO 30°F
10 TO 20°F
0 TO 10°F

© MQST

SPRING LOWS

AVERAGE LOW TEMPERATURE

60 TO 70°F
50 TO 60°F
40 TO 50°F
30 TO 40°F
20 TO 30°F
10 TO 20°F
0 TO 10°F

© MQST

SUMMER HIGHS

AVERAGE HIGH TEMPERATURE

ABOVE 110°F
100 TO 110°F
90 TO 100°F
80 TO 90°F
70 TO 80°F
60 TO 70°F
50 TO 60°F

© MQST

SUMMER LOWS

AVERAGE LOW TEMPERATURE

90 TO 100°F
80 TO 90°F
70 TO 80°F
60 TO 70°F
50 TO 60°F
40 TO 50°F
30 TO 40°F

© MQST

FALL HIGHS

AVERAGE HIGH TEMPERATURE

90 TO 100°F
80 TO 90°F
70 TO 80°F
60 TO 70°F
50 TO 60°F
40 TO 50°F
30 TO 40°F
20 TO 30°F

© MQST

FALL LOWS

AVERAGE LOW TEMPERATURE

70 TO 80°F
60 TO 70°F
50 TO 60°F
40 TO 50°F
30 TO 40°F
20 TO 30°F
10 TO 20°F

© MQST

GEORGE PARKS HIGHWAY

323 miles | **1½ days** | (N)

Road Notes
Linking the state's two largest cities – Anchorage and Fairbanks – with Denali National Park & Preserve, this highway travels through the kind of scenery that defines the Alaskan interior: tundra and muskeg, the continent's highest peaks, glaciers, forests, wild rivers, and lonely expanses inhabited only by moose, grizzlies, foxes, wolves, and a wealth of birds. Unless you enjoy subzero temperatures, come here during the brief bloom of the Alaskan summer, when daylight lasts as long as 21 hours.

Start near Wasilla (pg. 24, F7)

The George Parks Highway begins at its junction with the Glenn Highway and then heads west to Wasilla. For testimonials to the self-sufficiency and isolation of this area's old-time bush communities in the days before the Parks was built, visit the Dorothy G. Page Museum (907.373.9071). The nearby Iditarod Trail Committee Headquarters (907.376.5155) has a museum and sled-dog rides.

Leaving Wasilla, the highway soon picks up the Little Susitna River (mile 57.1), thronged by migrating salmon in late spring and midsummer. At mile 70.8 the Willow Creek Parkway offers access to riverside wetlands flanking the Susitna River's Delta Islands. Hatcher Pass Junction Road at mile 71.2 leads to the Willow Creek State Recreation Area (907.745.3975), noted for its

profusion of wildflowers.

Weather permitting, northbound views of 20,320-foot Mount McKinley, the highest peak in North America, begin about mile 76. Also called Denali—meaning the "high one" in an Athapaskan dialect – the peak rises 15,000 feet above the surrounding terrain.

Exit at mile 98.7 and follow the 14.5-mile road to Talkeetna, now a popular staging area for climbing expeditions to Mount McKinley. About 28 miles north of the Talkeetna turnoff, the highway enters Denali State Park (907.745.3975). This primitive 324,240-acre state preserve shares the natural wonders but not the crowds of the adjoining national park.

Few McKinley views match the one from the turnout at mile 135.2, where signs identify various Alaska Range landmarks. In another 20 miles you will be able to see Eldridge Glacier, just six miles west of the road. Turnouts along here lead to creeks, beaver ponds, and good fishing spots.

At mile 174, the road crosses the bridge above 260-foot-deep Hurricane Gulch, then continues north to Broad Pass (mile 201.3), whose summit marks a watershed divide: From here, north-flowing streams drain into the Yukon River and south-flowing into Cook Inlet.

Traffic builds near the entrance to Denali National Park & Preserve (mile 237.3; 907.683.2294). North of the park entrance, the highway negotiates the steep Nenana River Canyon. Scan the heights above Moody Bridge (mile 242.9) for Dall sheep.

In the sleepy town of Nenana (mile 304.5), the highway rejoins the Nenana River at its confluence with the 440-mile Tanana River.

Between Nenana and Fairbanks, far horizons suggest the scale of Alaskan terrain. The plain extending west from mile 318 includes Minto Flats Game Refuge (907.459.7289), a primordially pristine wildlife sanctuary. The Parks ends near downtown Fairbanks (907.456.5774), at the junction with Route 2.

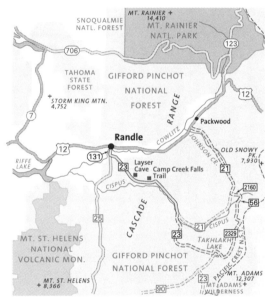
Denali National Park & Preserve

MOUNT ADAMS DRIVE

67 miles | **4 hours** | (N)

Road Notes
This drive in southern Washington feels almost like a hike, as it follows a series of paved and unpaved roads deep into the Gifford Pinchot National Forest. Along the way, it passes lakes, rivers and creeks, old-growth forests, and memorable mountain views. Don't hurry through this beautiful country – there are a number of good campsites right along the roadside, and if you have basic backpacking gear the road runs past trailheads with access to the subalpine wildflower meadows and mountain views of the Mount Adams and Goat Rocks Wildernesses.

Start at Randle (pg. 134, J9)

From Randle, turn south on Route 131. After going two miles, make a left turn onto Cispus Road. You'll pass a bucolic blend of small ranches, farms, and orchards for several miles until

you cross into the Gifford Pinchot National Forest (Randle Ranger District, 360.497.1100; Packwood Ranger District, 360.494.0600).

Once in the national forest, the drive, now FR 23, tunnels through

a classic western Cascades old-growth forest that is anchored by massive Douglas firs. To appreciate the size of these evergreen skyscrapers, walk up to one. Its trunk will be bigger across than you are tall.

Hiking trails branch off FR 23 in this area; stretch your legs on the quarter-mile Camp Creek Falls Trail, seven or eight miles from the Layser Cave turnoff. Camp Creek Falls itself plunges 30 feet over a rocky ledge, and along the trail, you might see a six-inch banana slug chomping on leaves, or a newt stepping in slow motion across the forest floor.

From here, the road soon picks up the Cispus River. For the next 15 miles, you stay with the river as it meanders down the valley. You'll see a snow-draped peak in the southeast; that's Mount Adams, the 12,307-foot volcano for which this route is named.

A couple of miles farther on, you leave FR 23 and turn left onto FR 2329, which soon brings you to Takhlakh Lake. The large, tree-lined lake – one of Washington's

best camping spots – is exquisitely backdropped by Mount Adams. Just beyond the lake is the trailhead for the five-mile path to Adams Creek / Killen Creek Meadows, a beautiful high-country area that's ablaze with wildflowers all summer.

FR 2329 then follows along the northern edge of the Mount Adams Wilderness. Along the way, Mount Adams frequently punctuates the southern sky, while 14,410-foot Mount Rainier

rises far to the north. Shimmering ribbons of icy, clear water flow from the nearby mountainsides.

Some ten miles past Takhlakh Lake, turn right onto FR 56 and follow it along the Cispus River for about a mile, then turn left on FR 2160. After two miles, turn right on FR 21. Passing several more groves of enormous Douglas firs, the road tightropes along a mountainside high above Johnson Creek for several miles before it ends at the junction with U.S. 12.

Mount Rainier

ROGUE UMPQUA SCENIC BYWAY

120 miles | **½ day** | (N)

Road Notes
This byway in southwest Oregon offers the rare opportunity to drive alongside two of the country's federally designated Wild and Scenic Rivers – the North Umpqua and the Rogue – both a feast of rapids, waterfalls, gorges, and serene stretches of cold, clear mountain water. These rivers are the stuff of fly-fishing legend, with salmon and steelhead runs that still bear some resemblance to the explosion of life that Zane Grey made famous in the 1930s with his stories. Both rivers are favorites with white-water rafters as well. Also on the itinerary is spectacular Crater Lake National Park. Summer is the prime time to experience all of these southern Oregon experiences, and at Crater Lake in particular you should be prepared for crowds.

Start at Roseburg (pg. 110, J3)

From the quiet town of Roseburg, head east on Route 138. For the next 16 miles the road passes through farmland on its way to the North Umpqua River, which

stages a dramatic entrance in the town of Glide. Below the town's Colliding Rivers Viewpoint, the North Umpqua and the Little River meet.

Leaving Glide, the road follows the North Umpqua up into the forests of the Cascade Range. A half mile beyond mile 21.5, stop at Swiftwater Park. The 79-mile North Umpqua Trail, good for backpacking and mountain biking, begins across the river here.

Among fly-fishing enthusiasts the next 30 miles of the North Umpqua are world famous for summer steelhead runs. Much of this stretch is framed by the towering basaltic cliffs of the North Umpqua River Canyon. Some nine miles past Swiftwater Park you enter the Umpqua National Forest (541.672.6601). Trails are plentiful here, often leading to waterfalls. Near the Toketee Ranger Station, the gorgeous half-mile trail to 120-foot-high Toketee Falls winds

above a narrow, rocky gorge resounding with the North Umpqua's turbulence. The trail ends at a viewing platform high above the falls.

About 18 miles farther on, a detour takes you to capacious Diamond Lake, backdropped by thick coniferous forests and the snow-covered peaks of the Cascades, including 8,363-foot Mount Bailey. A detour of about two miles on Route 138 leads to Crater Lake National Park (541.594.2211). Inky blue Crater Lake, the deepest lake in the nation, fills the caldera of dormant Mount Mazama.

To continue, bear right off Route 230. In three miles, you'll enter the Rogue River National Forest (541.858.2200). For a view of the Crater's rim, stop at Crater

Rim Viewpoint, a couple of miles into the national forest.

For about the next 20 miles, Route 230 descends past trees and occasional lava flows almost two million years old; dropping into the canyon of the Rogue River (541.479.3735), the road meanders alongside the river. Route 230 soon ends, and you join Route 62 south. In 1.5 miles you'll come to Union Creek, a historic Civilian Conservation Corps center that is now a tiny hamlet. At Natural Bridge, a mile south of Union Creek, another short trail offers more great views of the Rogue. At one point, the river actually disappears underground for some 200 feet through another ancient lava tube.

Continuing four more miles through stands of looming sugar pines, ponderosa pines, and Douglas firs, the road passes Mammoth Pines Nature Trail.

The drive ends about six miles farther on, when it enters the small logging town of Prospect.

Rogue River, Crater Lake National Park

65 miles | 2 hours

CALIFORNIA

LOST COAST

Road Notes

The Lost Coast is California's longest completely undeveloped stretch of wild shoreline, and its hallmarks – steeply pitched mountains rising out of the sea, clad with dense old-growth redwoods and wreathed almost perpetually in thick fog – are more in keeping with the Pacific Northwest than with the sunny imagery we associate with the Golden State. Many of the natural wonders of this area are beyond the reach of the automobile; indeed, backpacking the cobblestoned, black-sand beaches of the Lost Coast is one of the most remote wilderness treks you can manage in the lower 48. However, driving this little-traveled road, and stopping in two interesting, friendly settlements, will give you a feel for the place.

Start at Ferndale (pg. 30, D3)

Begin in the Eel River Valley at Ferndale (707.786.4477), an 1852 town that grew rich from creameries. An ideally timed visit to Ferndale would coincide with May's World Champion Kinetic Sculpture Race, in which whimsically designed human-powered vehicles compete over a course that travels both land and water.

Follow Mattole Road out of town, zigzagging up slopes wooded with maples and evergreens. After four miles, a wide view opens across forested valleys, then grassy hills appear. This stretch is called Wildcat Ridge, but the animals you're likely to see are hawks overhead and cows in the windswept pastures. The road descends to the Bear River and a ranch at Capetown, a former stage stop. A precipitous stretch continues on to Cape Mendocino. Here, three large tectonic plates grind together just off the coast, creating one of the continent's most active earthquake zones. For some five miles you drive beside a tidal zone that rose about four feet during the April 1992 earthquake, giving the appearance of a perpetual low tide.

Ahead, there's a five-mile side trip on Lighthouse Road to the shore; from there, a 3.5-mile trail leads to an old lighthouse. Here, at the mouth of the Mattole River, is where backpackers set out into the wilds of the Lost Coast; the southern terminus of the trek is the tiny fishing and vacation-home village of Shelter Cove. You're on the northern margin of the King Range National Conservation Area (707.986.7731), whose steep terrain, including 4,088-foot King Peak, defies highway engineers.

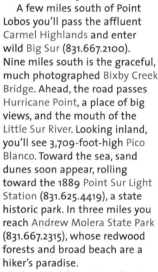

Humboldt Redwoods State Park

Return to Mattole Road and drive on to Honeydew, no more than a store yawning in the shade. The road climbs, crossing the Mattole and then Panther Gap as you enter Humboldt Redwoods State Park (707.946.2263) and Rockefeller Forest, which hold more than 40 percent of the world's remaining old-growth redwoods. Because some sections of the Avenue of the Giants have been turned into commercial tourist attractions, you may want to consider getting into the backcountry of this park, where there are plenty of old-growth trees in their primeval state. The Eel River, an excellent canoeing and fishing stream that has numerous swimming holes, runs through the park.

Ahead, in South Fork, the road joins U.S. 101 and Avenue of the Giants. The latter, one of the most famous scenic routes in the country, runs from Phillipsville north to Pepperwood and will take you through touristy hamlets, magnificent forests, and yes, even a living redwood you can drive your car through.

123 miles | 6 hours

CALIFORNIA

CALIFORNIA 1 SOUTH

Road Notes

Along this coastline, central California preserves its natural beauty and remembers its roots. The drive starts in historic Monterey, visits the art colony of Carmel, and threads through Big Sur, where the rocky, chaparral peaks of the Santa Lucias plunge into the Pacific in one of the planet's most dramatic encounters between land and sea. Overnighting amid Big Sur's towering redwoods is popular, but both beds and campsites are scarce – make reservations well in advance. Farther south, the landscape mellows to oak-studded hills as the road passes Hearst Castle on its way to Morro Bay. Temperatures are cool along the coast year round; winter sees more rain, and summer often brings thick coastal fog.

Start at Monterey (pg. 32, P7)

Join Route 1 in Monterey (831.649.1770). Visit touristy Fisherman's Wharf and Cannery Row, home of the celebrated Monterey Bay Aquarium (831.648.4888), where the world's largest window (15 feet high by 54 feet long) looks onto an indoor ocean. Also worth taking in is the Path of History, a tour of historic adobe buildings that celebrates Monterey's heritage as a fishing boomtown and capital of Spanish California.

Big Sur coastline

Drive three miles south on Route 1 to Carmel-by-the-Sea (831.624.2522), an upscale village of quaint cottages, inns, restaurants, art galleries, and shops. From Carmel, drive 3.5 miles south to the magical Point Lobos State Reserve (831.624.4909), which encompasses coves, rocky headlands, meadows, and the nation's first undersea ecological reserve. On land, trails offer sightings of black-tailed deer, playful sea otters, and noisy sea lions.

A few miles south of Point Lobos you'll pass the affluent Carmel Highlands and enter wild Big Sur (831.667.2100). Nine miles south is the graceful, much photographed Bixby Creek Bridge. Ahead, the road passes Hurricane Point, a place of big views, and the mouth of the Little Sur River. Looking inland, you'll see 3,709-foot-high Pico Blanco. Toward the sea, sand dunes soon appear, rolling toward the 1889 Point Sur Light Station (831.625.4419), a state historic park. In three miles you reach Andrew Molera State Park (831.667.2315), whose redwood forests and broad beach are a hiker's paradise.

Along the five miles of urban Big Sur you'll pass the entrance to Pfeiffer Big Sur State Park (831.667.2315), with a large public campground and hiking trails that run past old-growth redwoods and cool swimming holes. A half mile beyond is Big Sur Station (831.667.2315), a backcountry information center. Next, keep your eyes peeled for an unmarked road (the second right after the station) leading west toward Pfeiffer Beach, where the surf roars through arched rocks.

After nearly two miles you reach Nepenthe (831.667.2345), a mountaintop restaurant famous for its jaw-dropping view. Another eight miles along is Julia Pfeiffer Burns State Park (831.667.2315), whose terrain ranges from 3,000-foot-high ridges to an underwater preserve.

After 35 miles of hairpin turns through southern Big Sur, the landscape settles down to hills and pastureland. Next stop is San Simeon, a staging area for the five-mile bus ride to Hearst Castle (805.927.2020).

Continue about seven miles to Cambria, an arty town nestled against hills; on the ocean side of the highway, at Moonstone Beach, look for moonstones and California jade. The route ends at Morro Bay (800.231.0592), easily identified by its landmark Morro Rock, an ancient volcanic cone.

27 miles | 2 hours

ARIZONA

OAK CREEK CANYON DRIVE

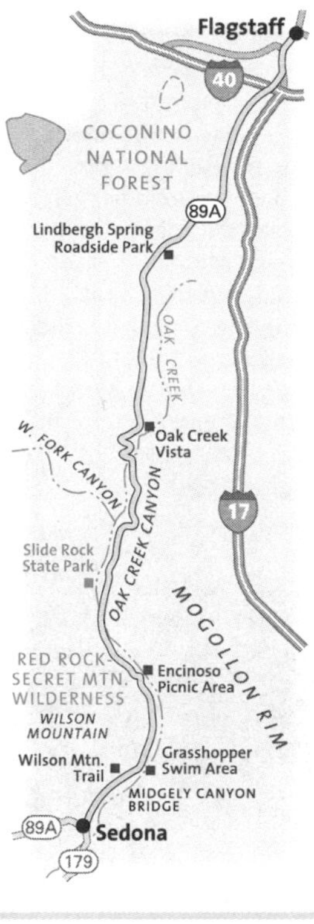

Road Notes

On the southern edge of the great Colorado Plateau that produced such marvels as Grand, Zion, and Bryce Canyons lies an equally stunning, but far more intimate spot – Oak Creek Canyon. For the past three million years, Oak Creek has carved a 12-mile-long, 2,000-foot-deep slice along the fault line into the ancient geologic past. From the ponderosa pines of Flagstaff to the red-rock desertscape of Sedona, the Oak Creek Canyon Drive reveals layers of dazzling red sandstone, tan limestone, and purple siltstone, all eroded into curious shapes. The numerous camping and picnic grounds along the short route are very popular – come in fall, when the crowds have thinned and the cottonwoods turn a fiery yellow.

Start at Flagstaff (pg. 26, F8)

Route 89A leaves the bustle of Flagstaff, a former lumber town in the shadows of the rugged San Francisco Mountains, and travels through the thick ponderosa pines of the Coconino National Forest (520.527.3600). After three miles the road passes the small Lindbergh Spring Roadside Park, a good spot for a close-up look at ponderosas. Their clusters of three long needles distinguish them from other pine species.

After eight miles atop the plateau, the road comes to the Oak Creek Vista on the left, at the lip of a great escarpment known as the Mogollon Rim. Thirty million years ago, seismic forces thrust this section of the earth's crust thousands of feet above the surrounding land.

A short loop trail, where Native Americans sell crafts, brings you to the edge of a sheer drop. From this 6,400-foot vantage point, you'll see a diversity of plant life resulting from the dramatic elevation changes and relative abundance of water. Water-loving trees, such as alder, willow, oak, and walnut, thrive along the creek. Dense brush dominates the dry hillsides. Where the canyon widens, desert plants appear.

From the overlook, the road – which began as a cattle trail and was later adapted to wagons – switchbacks precipitously downward for two miles to the Pumphouse Wash Bridge. About 17 miles south of Flagstaff, a day-use area leads to the canyon's most popular hike, the West Fork Trail, a moderate three-mile walk under sheer walls into West Fork Canyon, past fern forests and sandy beaches.

The road continues, passing campsites and picnic grounds along the Oak Creek. Above, layers of sedimentary rock mark the rock walls. In age and composition they are like the rocks in the top third of the Grand Canyon.

Halfway through the canyon drive, Slide Rock State Park (520.282.3034) appears on the right. Beyond the orchard and down some steps, a path leads to the site of the park's most popular activity. Here, the creek bubbles through a shoot of smooth Coconino sandstone, and the air fills with shouts as people ride the natural slide. (Be sure to bring water socks and jeans – the ride can be bumpy.) In summer you must arrive before 11 a.m. to park.

Red Rock Crossing, Coconino National Forest

Not far beyond Slide Rock is Oak Creek's other popular swim spot, Grasshopper Swim Area, with deep pools and soaring cliffs.

Just after this swim area, a pull-off on the north side of Midgely Bridge serves as the trailhead for the Wilson Mountain Trail, which pushes west into the Red Rocks–Secret Mountain Wilderness. Though strenuous – the trail rises 2,300 feet in 5.6 miles – the spectacular views extend several hundred miles and encompass Verde Valley, Sedona, and Oak Creek Canyon. An equally strenuous alternative is the North Wilson Trail, which starts north of the Encinoso Picnic Area and joins the Wilson Mountain Trail. Two miles from Midgely Bridge, the road passes out of the canyon and into Sedona, an arts community set among spectacular red-rock formations.

CA 30
CA 156
CA 30
CA 156
AZ 26
AZ 156

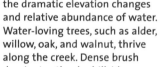

GILA SCENIC BYWAY

118 miles	½ day	

NEW MEXICO

Road Notes
Within the high-desert forests of Gila National Forest, this southwestern New Mexico route penetrates some of the nation's largest and most remote tracts of wilderness. It passes a couple of Old West towns, winds to ancient cliff dwellings, and skirts an immense open-pit copper mine. The tortuous road is all but impassable to RVs and trailers, and is slow going for anyone – make an early start to ensure you'll have time to explore the cliff dwellings.

Start at Silver City (pg. 93, L3)

The route begins at Silver City, a mining town that boomed in the 1870s, when silver was discovered. The town's colorful history is told at the Silver City Museum (505.538.5921).

From town, the route climbs north on Route 15 for six miles into the Pinos Altos Range and reaches the town of Pinos Altos, or "tall pines," which hugs the Continental Divide at 7,840 feet.

The famous bar at the Buckhorn Saloon (505.538.9911), which also has a fine restaurant, keeps the sleepy town alive.

After Pinos Altos the road narrows considerably as it winds through the Pinos Altos Range, heading up Cherry Creek past a couple of rustic picnic areas shaded by ponderosa pines and cottonwoods. Eighteen miles after Pinos Altos, the route drops steeply to Sapillo Creek, where Route 15 intersects with Route 35. Continue north for 17 miles to the Gila Cliff Dwellings National Monument. On its way up to the cliff dwellings, the road climbs through a series of switchbacks, passing the Senator Clinton P. Anderson Wilderness Overlook after about six miles. The Gila River Canyon lies 2,000 feet below, while spectacular vistas of the Gila Wilderness spread to the horizon. After the overlook, Route 15 crosses a level ridge with open views and then descends sharply to a bridge across the Gila River.

Four miles later, the road reaches Gila Cliff Dwellings

National Monument (505.536.9344). The road to the dwellings passes the Lower Scorpion Campground, which features a small cave dwelling. (The short paved path to the right ends at a series of ancient red pictographs.) Parking for the major cliff dwellings lies just beyond the campground. A one-mile loop climbs 175 feet to the dwellings on the southeast-facing cliff. Five caves contain a remarkable series of 42 rooms. Some 40 to 50 Mogollon people lived in these dwellings in the late 13th century.

Retrace the route to Sapillo Creek and take Route 35 southeast for four miles to pine-hemmed Lake Roberts. As the road winds around the lake, it passes Vista Village, an archaeological site undergoing excavation. It's believed that prehistoric Native Americans occupied an 18- to 25-room pueblo here. The road continues up a wide valley and again crests the Continental Divide before reaching the Mimbres River Valley and the

Gila National Forest

Mimbres Ranger District (505.536.2250) outside the town of Mimbres.

Near the town of San Lorenzo, the route intersects Route 152, which heads west 8.5 miles to the overlook of the Phelps Dodge Santa Rita Copper Mine, an immense hole in the earth. Continue on to Santa Clara, where U.S. 180 takes you back to Silver City.

TALIMENA SCENIC BYWAY

54 miles	2 hours	

OKLAHOMA/ARKANSAS

Road Notes
Built in the late 1960s expressly for grand views, this two-lane highway ripples over the gentle Ouachita Mountains, which straddle the Oklahoma-Arkansas border. Evergreen and deciduous trees shoulder the road, the latter making for gorgeous floral displays in spring and brilliant color in autumn. The byway's name derives from a combination of the towns that form its two endpoints – Talihina and Mena. It runs through the 1.7-million-acre Ouachita National Forest (501.321.5202), the South's oldest (established in 1907) and largest national forest. Ouachita is a Native American word meaning either "good hunting grounds" or "hunting trip," and these woods still hold plentiful deer, squirrel, and other wildlife.

Start at Talihina (pg. 109, H18)

Begin in Talihina, a town founded by missionaries in the late 1880s, when the Frisco Railway came through the mountains (its name is Choctaw for "iron road"). A Visitor Information Station about seven miles to the northeast, at the junction of U.S. 271 and Oklahoma 1, marks the start of the designated byway. Just 0.3 mile past the information station you come to Choctaw Vista, on the west end of Winding Stair Mountain, part of the Ouachita Mountains. From here you can look out on the beautiful dark blue hills and valleys through which the

Choctaw traveled west from Mississippi, in compliance with the 1830 Indian Removal Act.

For the next several miles the road cuts through a forest of shortleaf pine and scrub oak. The east-west lay of the Ouachita Mountains has created separate plant communities on either side: Post oak, blackjack, and serviceberry cover southern slopes, while the rich soil of the northern slopes supports white oak, hickory, dogwood, and papaw.

Past the forest entrance, stop at Panorama Vista for sweeping views of the mountains and the small farming villages tucked

into the Holson Valley. Hang-glider enthusiasts often launch from here. Golden eagles, vultures, and hawks also soar on the updrafts.

Continue on to Horse Thief Springs (mile 16). The road now swoops back and forth down Winding Stair Mountain, giving you constantly shifting views. The Ouachita Mountains once extended to the Appalachians, before the Mississippi separated the ranges. The 300-million-year-old sandstones and shales

Winding Stair Mountain

of the Ouachitas were thrust up, folded, and faulted. Fault lines are visible in places along the drive, including the area around Robert S. Kerr Arboretum and Nature Center.

For several miles past the nature center the byway follows the crest of Rich Mountain through a forest of dwarf oak stunted by severe ice storms and southerly winds. Oklahoma 1 changes to Arkansas 88 as you cross the state line. At about mile 40, the Old Pioneer

Cemetery holds the graves of 23 people who homesteaded here between the mid-19th and mid-20th centuries.

Two miles beyond, the Queen Wilhelmina State Park (501.394.2863) features dramatic southerly views from the crest of Rich Mountain. The park centers around a rustic stone lodge. Originally constructed at the turn of the century and since rebuilt, the lodge was named for the queen of Holland, whose country held a substantial stake in the local railroad.

Three miles east of the park stands the highest point on the drive, Rich Mountain Fire Tower (2,681 feet). From this vantage, you have fine views of the forested mountains.

The drive ends in Mena, a timber and cattle town that sprang to life in 1896 when the first train of the Kansas City Southern Railroad came chugging through the mountains.

SAN JUAN SKYWAY

236 miles	1-2 days	

COLORADO

Road Notes
As its fanciful name implies, the San Juan Skyway flirts with the heights, climbing to more than 10,000 feet three times as it charts a ragged loop through the mountains and high deserts of southwestern Colorado. Starting at Ridgway, this spectacular route heads south over the crest of the San Juan Mountains and passes through historic mining towns, red-rock canyons, and Mesa Verde National Park, where you can walk through 800-year-old Ancestral Puebloan cliff dwellings. The drive is beautiful year-round, but keep in mind that the mountain passes close sometimes after heavy winter snows.

Start at Ridgway S.P. (pg. 38, J7)

Begin four miles north of town, at Ridgway State Park (970.626.5822), where U.S. 550 tops a dry hill and the southern skyline fills with the jagged crest of the San Juans. Cross

the valley floor to Ridgway, at the base of 14,150-foot Mount Sneffels, then continue south along the Uncompahgre River.

At Ouray, multicolored cliffs squeeze the valley against the

base of 14,000-foot peaks. Ouray Hot Springs, a municipal pool, steams at the north end of downtown Ouray's ornate 1880s buildings. U.S. 550 next switchbacks up into the mountains, offering splendid vistas back down to Ridgway. Waterfalls and creeks spill from side canyons and high cliffs in Uncompahgre Gorge. Next, just drive up the short series of hairpin turns, top the rim of the gorge, and let your pulse soar. Vivid crimson peaks burst into view, with

broad smears of orange and red gravel streaming down into the dark surrounding evergreens. It's an astonishing, surrealistic sight, and yet the peaks carry mundane labels: Red Mountain No. 1, No. 2, and No. 3. You climb nearly to tree line before arriving at 11,008-foot Red Mountain Pass, and then the road begins its ten-mile, 1,700-foot descent into Silverton.

Continuing south, the road winds along the contours of the mountains to Coal Bank Pass,

then tilts downward toward the plateau and canyon country around Durango, an 1880s railroad town. From Durango, follow U.S. 160 west through a rolling terrain of minor canyons and mesas. About eight miles beyond Mancos is Mesa Verde National Park (970.529.4465).

Continue along U.S. 160 toward Cortez, then turn north onto Route 145, which follows the Dolores River back into the San Juan Mountains. About ten miles from Rico, you'll see 13,113-foot Lizard Head Peak off to the left. Lizard Head Pass (10,222 feet) offers more incredible views of the San Juans, then the road descends over some miles to a T-intersection. Turn right and drive into Telluride. Its mint Victorian downtown is nestled in a pocket valley beneath the San Juans, and 365-foot Bridal Veil Falls drops from the cliffs behind town. Follow Route 145 to Placerville, turn right on Route 62, and after crossing the pass of Dallas Divide, you'll glide back down to Ridgway.

San Juan Mountains

122 miles	½–1 day	

UTAH 12 SCENIC BYWAY

Road Notes
Some of Utah's most outstanding high-desert scenery unfolds along this route, which begins near the pale orange spires of Bryce Canyon and ends amid the immense sandstone domes of Capitol Reef. Between these two national parks, this remote highway snakes along narrow ridge tops, carves through red-rock canyons past prehistoric Native American ruins, and ascends 11,000-foot Boulder Mountain for breathtaking views.

Start near Dixie N.F. (pg. 129, 55)

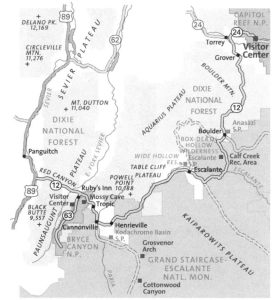

From its western terminus at U.S. 89, Route 12 soon enters Dixie National Forest (435.865.3700) and rolls through Red Canyon, a fairylike world of sculptured limestone formations colored brilliant red by iron oxides and accented by ponderosa pines.

At 12 miles, Route 63 branches off to the south and enters Bryce Canyon National Park (435.834.5322). The road along the rim skirts 12 huge amphitheaters that drop a thousand feet.

Back on Route 12, the next stop, about 13 miles past the small town of Tropic, is a pullout with stunning views of the salmon-colored cliffs of 10,188-foot Powell Point. The road continues east across Table Cliff Plateau and reaches Escalante State Park and Visitor Center (435.826.4466). Wide Hollow Reservoir offers trout fishing, while a 1.5-mile nature trail leads to a petrified forest and a view of the early Mormon town of Escalante.

Highway 12 next crosses Calf Creek near the Calf Creek Campground (435.826.5499), where a 5.5-mile trail leads to 126-foot Calf Creek Falls. In this area, the road twists along the crest of a narrow ridge with spectacular views of Calf Creek far below. Continue on six miles to Boulder, where Anasazi State Park (435.335.7308) offers a re-created dwelling and a museum of the Anasazi, who, along with the Fremont Indians, occupied this region in prehistoric times.

North of Boulder, Route 12 enters a landscape of sagebrush and piñon pines. It ascends Boulder Mountain, which sits on the Aquarius Plateau, one of the continent's highest timbered plateaus. In fall, stands of fire-yellow aspens play against the evergreens. Views from several overlooks, such as Point Lookout, are exceptional. The road descends to the junction with Route 24 near Torrey.

Red Canyon, Dixie National Forest

Turn right onto Route 24 and enter Capitol Reef National Park (435.425.3791), which preserves a portion of the Waterpocket Fold, a great wrinkle in the earth's crust. Exposed edges of the uplift have eroded into a dramatic slickrock wilderness of massive domes, cliffs, and a maze of twisted canyons. Stop at the Visitor Center to plan your park visit.

UT 128

UT 164

---

184 miles	½ day	

SALMON RIVER SCENIC ROUTE

Road Notes
This scenic route follows central Idaho's largest river north from its headwaters in the Sawtooth Range through desert canyons to the tiny town of North Fork, where the waters swerve suddenly to the west and leave all roads far behind. The drive then heads back into the mountains, following the path of Lewis and Clark over Lost Trail Pass and down into the Bitterroot Valley. It's a gorgeous drive and one that touches on major historical themes – exploration, fur trapping, mining, settlement, and Native American conflicts.

Start at Stanley (pg. 51, J4)

The route begins in Stanley, in full view of Idaho's most spectacular peaks. Paralleling the Salmon River Route 75 slants down into a forested gorge lined with granite outcroppings. The river drops 15 feet a mile, charging through rapids and sweeping past hot-spring pools. The best known, Sunbeam Hot Springs, trickles down a rocky slope about 11 miles from Stanley. Less than a mile beyond the springs, the river stalls out in deep pools of emerald green at the crossroads town of Sunbeam.

Follow the river 2.5 miles east to Indian Riffles. The road continues along the Salmon River through small canyons that widen as you descend. Beyond Clayton, the river bends northeast and runs through a valley surrounded by high-desert hills.

Approaching the junction with U.S. 93, you pass under a towering cliff of rust-colored rock. Bighorn sheep frequent the area. A sign at the Bison Jump Archaeological Site describes how Native Americans drove small herds of the animals over the cliff.

At the junction of Route 75 and U.S. 93, stop at the Land of the Yankee Fork Visitor Center (208.879.5244) to see exhibits on the region's geology, history, and mining methods.

Soon you cross the Pahsimeroi River and round the northern flank of the Lemhi Range. About 18 miles past Challis, both road and river punch through a narrow gorge that widens into a spectacular canyon whose walls soar hundreds of feet.

Follow U.S. 93 to Salmon, an 1860s mining town and now a center for ranchers, loggers, and river runners. Heading north, the road runs through yet another canyon carved by the Salmon. Look for great blue herons, cliff swallows, deer, pronghorn, and maybe even river otters. At North Fork the river plunges west into the Salmon River Canyon and rushes across the vast wilderness of central Idaho.

U.S. 93 tunnels through dense forests to Lost Trail Pass, 7,014 feet, named in 1805 by the bewildered northbound party of Lewis and Clark. In 1877, during their epic flight for freedom, the Nez Perce also crossed east through these mountains. At the Big Hole National Battlefield (15 miles east on Route 43; 406.689.3205), you can walk over the ground where the Nez Perce beat back the U.S. Army.

From the pass, you descend into Bitterroot Valley. Stop at Indian Trees Campground to admire stands of mature ponderosa pines. The drive ends in Darby.

MT 84

ID 51

MT 160

ID 158

Salmon River, Sawtooth Range

---

162 miles	1 day	

CENTENNIAL SCENIC BYWAY

Road Notes
One of the finest drives in the Rockies, the Centennial Scenic Byway charts a long, doglegging course through the mountains and river valleys of northwest Wyoming. Along the way, it passes nearly every major sight in the region – the Wind River Range, the Tetons, the Snake River, and the Green River Valley. Get an early start so you can catch the morning light on the Tetons and still make Pinedale in time to watch the sun set on the Winds. The drive is spectacular year-round, though winter snows occasionally close Togwotee Pass.

Start at Dubois (pg. 140, E9)

The byway begins at Dubois, where the surrounding terrain shifts from colorful badlands to forested mountain slopes. As U.S. 26 climbs from town, look to the northeast to see 11,635-foot Ramshorn Peak, part of the volcanic Absaroka Range. Beside the road, the Wind River curves over beds of cobblestones, sliding past evergreens and aspens. About 20 miles from town, the Pinnacle Buttes burst over the treetops. Stop at Falls Campground to stroll the rim of the waterfall.

U.S. 26 rises steadily through a pine forest. In meadows rife with wildflowers, be on the lookout for moose, elk, deer, even bear. Soon, you cross Togwotee Pass (9,658 feet) and descend to Teton Range Overlook, with its incomparable view of Wyoming's best known mountains.

Drive out of the mountains onto the floodplain of the Buffalo Fork River, and you're soon in Grand Teton National Park (307.739.3600). At Moran Junction, Route 26 turns south and passes through a wetland area. Look for moose, elk, and bison along here. Continue south to the Snake River Overlook, with one of the classic views of the Teton Range. Bald eagles and ospreys sometimes glide over the river. From here, the drive heads south through Jackson Hole to Moose Junction, where you'll find the main park Visitor Center (307.739.3399). About six miles south of Moose, a fence encloses the National Elk Refuge, where nearly 10,000 elk gather every winter. Sleigh rides among the elk (307.733.0277) start from refuge headquarters.

Soon you arrive in Jackson, a former ranch town turned tourist mecca. Avoid the town's traffic by taking the truck route and follow U.S. 189/191 south. Seven miles from Jackson you'll hit the Snake River; follow it to Hoback Junction. Here, the Hoback River joins the Snake, and their combined waters send raging white water through the Grand Canyon of the Snake River.

Southeast of Bondurant, the road drops out of the mountains onto the sagebrush flats of the Green River Valley. Stop at the Museum of the Mountain Man (307.367.4101), on Route 189/191. End your tour by following Fremont Lake Road out of Pinedale to Fremont Lake.

WY 140

WY 165

Snake River, Grand Teton National Park

ND
103

ND
162

| 14 miles | ¾ hour | |

NORTH DAKOTA

Road Notes
Meandering through the magnificent badlands of western North Dakota so beloved by Theodore Roosevelt, this park road traverses the length of the 24,000-acre North Unit of the Theodore Roosevelt National Park. Traffic tends to be light for a national park, and you have ample opportunities for viewing wide prairies, wildlife, and, above all, the wonderful badlands rock formations. Pullouts en route have interpretive plaques and hiking trails.

Start at the Visitor Center (pg. 103, D2)

OXBOW OVERLOOK SCENIC BYWAY

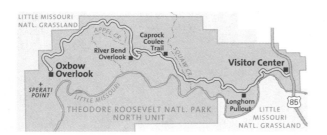

The drive begins at the Theodore Roosevelt National Park visitor center (701.623.4466), a worthwhile stop with good displays and films and a friendly staff. The park was named for the man whose experiences in North Dakota helped mold him into a world leader. Roosevelt first visited the badlands in 1883 to hunt bison and other big game. A vigorous conservationist, he set aside a tremendous amount of land for parks, forests, and wildlife refuges during his terms

as President (1901–9).

The Longhorn Pullout (mile 2) is situated on the edge of a prairie where a small herd of longhorn steer graze. Longhorn in the area date from an 1884 Texas trail drive that pushed 4,000 head into an open range vacated by dwindling bison. Thousands of longhorn followed in subsequent drives, but in 20 years they too had gone, victims of overgrazing and hard winters.

The scenery that captured Roosevelt's imagination is evident

at every bend in the road. Climbing through hills laced with juniper trees, the road soars above the canyons and ravines characteristic of the badlands. Watch for wildlife, often not far from the road–mule deer, prairie dogs, bison, and more. The Caprock Coulee Nature Trail (mile 7) takes about an hour (or longer if you make a loop) and offers an up-close examination of the local geology. Interpretive brochures are available at the trailhead.

River Bend Overlook (about mile 8) affords splendid views of peaks and rounded buttes and the cottonwood-lined Little Missouri far below. The multicolored rock formations are layers of sandstone, clay, shale, and petrified wood deposited millions of years ago. Easily eroded by the elements, the rocks have infinitely varied shapes – from drip castles to capped pillars and buttes. In 1864, Gen. Alfred Sully described the region as "hell with the fires out." The fires sometimes still burn when seams of lignite coal catch fire

Theodore Roosevelt National Park

from lightning and bake the surrounding clay a sienna red.

The road ends at Oxbow Overlook, another breathtaking vantage point. Here you can see where the Little Missouri once

flowed north toward Hudson Bay. Forced by a glacier to find a new course, the river turned east to the Mississippi during the last ice age.

SD
119

SD
163

| 33 miles | 1½ hours | |

SOUTH DAKOTA

Road Notes
First-time visitors to southwestern South Dakota will probably experience an odd sense of déjà vu. It's an elemental Old West landscape, and we have been here before– through the magic of the movies, anyway. The bison you'll see during this drive through the heart of the Black Hills may have been extras in *Dances With Wolves*, and amid the hoodoos and ponderosa pines it's easy to sense the lingering presence of the legends who once walked this land – Crazy Horse, Wild Bill Hickok and Calamity Jane, and Colonel Custer are a few. Today the most colorful time to be here is in August, when more than 100,000 Harley-Davidson enthusiasts stream into the area to attend the Sturgis Motorcycle Rally and Races.

Start at Wind Cave Natl. Park (pg. 119, F2)

CUSTER SCENIC BYWAY

Throughout history, the Black Hills, called Paha Sapa ("hills that are black") by the Lakota, were sacred ground to the Cheyenne, Arapaho, Kiowa, and Lakota – a

place to seek visions, to purify one's spirit, and a neutral site where warring tribes could meet. With the discovery of gold here in 1874, the passage of the Black

Hills from Native American to white hands ran its inevitable course. Colonel Custer and Sitting Bull, Little Bighorn and Wounded Knee are part of lasting American myth. There is still a strong Lakota presence in the area; they continue to fight in court to regain the Black Hills.

The drive begins at Wind Cave National Park (605.745.4600), where extensive subterranean architecture has been sculptured over the eons in the porous limestone surrounding the Black Hills. The 81-mile maze of caverns, only partially explored, are rife with interesting formations; guided tours are available. Above ground, in the park's mixed-grass prairies and pine forests, wildlife includes coyotes, bison, pronghorn, and mule deer.

Heading north along Route 87 from its junction with U.S. 385, stop at the Prairie Dog Pullout. If you stay in the car, you'll have more to watch; cars don't spook the rodents but people do. Farther along is Custer State Park (605.255.4515), contiguous with

the national park. The park has four jewellike lakes – Sylvan, Center, Stockade, and Legion Lakes – all offering swimming, fishing, boating, and camping.

Route 87 soon begins winding up through dense pine forest. Near Mount Coolidge you'll notice vast tracts of charred forest from the 1988 and 1990 fires that devastated the park. For a 360-degree panorama of the Black Hills, take the 1.3-mile gravel road (on the left) to Mount Coolidge Fire Tower.

The 14.5-mile section of Route 87 north of U.S. 16A is known as the Needles Highway (closed winters), and it's a thrilling finish to the drive. Around you rise the needles, or upthrust pylons of granite, in the heart of the Sioux holy land; amazing views seem magically to appear before your windshield. The drive ends at Sylvan Lake. Above its north shore rises Harney Peak, which, at 7,242 feet, is the highest mountain east of the Rockies.

Custer State Park

MO
82

MO
160

| 44 miles | 1 hour | |

MISSOURI

Road Notes
Coursing through the peaceful farm country and upland forests of southeastern Missouri, this winding road passes near a large section of the Mark Twain National Forest and crosses the Ozark National Scenic Riverways wilderness area. Protected in this wilderness are the Current and Jacks Fork Rivers, beautiful recreational rivers offering excellent fishing, canoeing, swimming, and camping opportunities. Most popular in spring and fall, the highway boasts redbud and dogwood trees in pink and white and a palette of brilliant autumn colors. Wildflowers, from last coldfront to first frost, enhance the beauty of the roadsides.

Start at Salem (pg. 82, J9)

MISSOURI OZARKS

From Salem, seat of Dent County, head south past the courthouse (on your left) on Route 19. The first several miles envelop you in the big, undulant pastures typical of the region. Roads at four and seven miles lead east to the Salem and Potosi Districts of the 1.5-million-acre Mark Twain National Forest (573.364.4621). If you take a right turn off Route 19 at the road at four miles, you'll be on your way west to Montauk State Park (573.548.2201), where seven cold springs form the headwaters of the Current River, which is regularly stocked with rainbow trout. The park has campsites, motel rooms, and cabins.

Back on Route 19 about ten miles from Salem, the wide, green fields begin yielding to thick forests. Cross Gladden Creek and continue on the windy road through shadowed glens and grassy meadows. A brief stretch of mobile homes and shacks gives way to woods and long views of the misty bluegreen Ozarks.

Traveling up now through the

hardwood forest, Route 19 ascends the Ozark Plateau, an eroded tableland spreading from northern Arkansas to southern Missouri and west to northeastern Oklahoma. Continue south into the Ozark National Scenic Riverways (573.323.4236), a National Park Service unit protecting more than 134 miles of the Current and Jacks Fork Rivers. A smooth, fast-flowing river with deep pools, the Current offers excellent bass

fishing and will be a memorable trip for novice canoeists and those who just want to float it on an inner tube.

Cross the sparkling Current River and make a left into the Round Spring campground and picnic area. Here you can explore one of the area's many caves, tucked into the high limestone bluff; park rangers offer a two-mile guided tour. Continue south as the road begins climbing again to good views of the valley

and hills. In about three miles you pass a tract of virgin pine. About nine miles farther, a pullout lets you savor the southern panorama of forested mountains. To get into the heart of these mountains, stop at Coldwater Ranch (573.226.3723) for guided horseback rides.

Route 19 next descends steeply to the Jacks Fork River; just beyond is the town of Eminence, which has outfitters for river expeditions and other activities. Five miles west of Eminence along Route 106 in Alley Spring is a one-room schoolhouse and a historic roller mill that used to grind corn and wheat. If you have time to continue on, check out the town of Van Buren, 21 miles southeast of Eminence via Route 19 and U.S. 60; there are more canoe- and tube-rental outfitters here, and a few miles south of town is Big Spring, the nation's largest single-outlet spring. It discharges 227 million gallons of water per day into the Current River.

Ozark National Scenic Riverways

---

150 miles	3 hours	

NORTH SHORE LAKE SUPERIOR DRIVE

MINNESOTA

Road Notes

Skirting the jagged, glacier-worn Sawtooth Mountains, this winding road follows the rocky shoreline of Lake Superior, passing lighthouses and cascading streams and penetrating the only part of the continental United States where a boreal forest ecology thrives. The route is at its best from spring through fall. The seaway is frozen throughout winter, a sublime sight for off-season travelers.

Start at Duluth (pg. 78, K11)

Grand Marais

Begin the drive in Duluth, and take in the eclectic mix of museums known as The Depot (218.727.8025), housed in a restored 1892 railway station. Head northeast on Route 61 (the old one, not the four-lane expressway). About four miles beyond downtown, at Lester River, walks, overlooks, and stairways reveal the lake's immensity.

Beyond Two Harbors, the road climbs, twists, and tunnels through Silver Cliff and Lafayette Bluff. Ancient volcanoes created the North Shore's bedrock, which was then sculpted by the same glaciers that carved out the Great Lakes. The centerpiece of Gooseberry Falls State Park (218.834.3855) – the first of eight extraordinary state parks along the drive – is a stunning cascade that tumbles into Lake Superior.

The road continues east to Split Rock Lighthouse State Park (218.226.6377), and its restored 1910 lighthouse. The Split Rock History Center (218.226.6372) has exhibits on shipwrecks and commercial lake fishing. Beyond Silver Bay, Tettegouche State Park (218.226.6365) has 17 miles of trails.

Continue on to Superior National Forest – home to moose, wolves, black bears, and loons – and then through Lutsen to Cascade River State Park

(218.387.3053).

About five miles ahead is Grand Marais and the beginning of the most magnificent stretch of this drive. A sense of remoteness envelops the road as it continues deeper into the realm of the early fur trappers and missionaries. Just past the second intersection with Route 14, the Moose Area sign marks one of the best spots to see these impressive animals.

The road continues through Hovland and enters the Grand Portage Indian Reservation, home of the Ojibwa. Regional lore is recounted at Grand Portage National Monument (218.387.2788).

Beyond Grand Portage, the road climbs to a crest near 1,348-foot Mount Josephine. From a scenic overlook take in superb views of the lake, the Susie Islands, and Wauswaugoning Bay. The drive continues across the international border into Canada, where it officially ends at Thunder Bay.

MN 78 · MN 160

---

96 miles	3 hours	

CHERRY ORCHARDS DRIVE

MICHIGAN

Road Notes

Prolific cherry trees, handsome summer resort towns, stunning fall foliage, and Lake Michigan vistas highlight this eastern lakeshore drive. Once trod by Indians, French fur traders, and Jesuit missionaries, the route is most enjoyable from spring through fall.

Start at Cross Village (pg. 74, G7)

From Cross Village, Route 119 begins a lovely 27-mile traverse that traces Michigan's rugged shoreline through an area known as l'arbre croche, the crooked tree, named by early voyageurs who used a lone gnarled fir on the shore as a landmark.

Just past a golf course is Harbor Springs, whose small downtown has a pleasant cluster of shops and restaurants. Nearby, Thorne Swift Nature Preserve (231.526.6401) offers a sampling of dunes, wetlands, and stands of trees. Route 119 wends southeast around Petoskey State Park (231.347.2311) and then ends. Continue west on U.S. 31 to Bay View, a charming Victorian town overlooking the bay. In Petoskey, an exhibit at the Little Traverse History Museum (231.347.2620) honors Ernest Hemingway, who spent 20 summers in the area.

When you see the tip of Lake Charlevoix, you'll know the community of Charlevoix is a short distance ahead. Hop aboard the two-and-a-quarter-hour ferry ride to Beaver Island (231.448.2505), in Lake Michigan, where you'll find sandy beaches, hiking trails, and the Marine Museum (231.448.2254).

As U.S. 31 continues south, the woods give way to rolling farmland and panoramic views of Grand Traverse Bay and the forested hills of Leelanau Peninsula. Just before Atwood

Charlevoix Lighthouse

there are groves of cherry trees.

North of the town of Torch Lake, look for Barnes County Park, located west on Barnes Park Road, with its secluded beach on Grand Traverse Bay. Get a close-up view of Torch Lake – once fished at night by Native Americans – by detouring east from U.S. 31 onto Barnes Road, about three miles south of town. Veer right on West Torch Lake Drive and follow it to Campbell Road, back to

U.S. 31. An M-DOT Roadside Park 2.5 miles south offers a spacious picnic spot at Birch Lake.

Detour at the lakeside resort town of Traverse City onto Route 37, which meanders north through the nation's greatest concentration of cherry trees, to the 1870 Old Mission Light, located just south of the 45th parallel – halfway between the Equator and the North Pole.

MI 74 · MI 159

---

53 miles	1 hour	

GREAT RIVER ROAD

WISCONSIN

Road Notes

Squeezing between steep, lush bluffs and the Mississippi River, this segment of the Great River Road (Route 35) passes through river towns dating back to before the days of steamboats and Mark Twain. The drive is at its most scenic during fall foliage.

Start at Prairie du Chien (pg. 139, Q4)

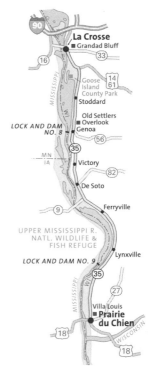

Begin at Prairie du Chien, a former outpost for French voyageurs, three miles north of the confluence of the Wisconsin and Mississippi Rivers. Visit Villa Louis (608.326.2721) and the Victorian palace, built in 1870, now a museum that includes an exhibit on the history of fur trading.

Outside city limits, Route 35 wanders through cornfields and dairy country. About five miles from the city, it wraps around high sandstone bluffs – forested with sumacs, sugar maples, and oaks. After about three miles the Mississippi appears, dotted with wooded islands that create a maze of marshes and ponds.

The rich bottomland is home to a wide variety of birds, mammals, and fish species. Protected by the Upper Mississippi River National Wildlife and Fish Refuge (507.452.4232), it stretches 260 miles from Wabasha, Minnesota to Rock Island, Illinois.

About six miles north, Lock and Dam Number 9 creates a beautiful pool that edges close to the bluffs, with the road snaking between. Similar pools to the north make this a virtually continuous lakeside drive.

Over the next 40 miles, Route 35 passes through a string of fishing villages, including Ferryville, perhaps the nation's longest one-street village, and De Soto, named for the Spanish explorer who crossed the Mississippi in the 1540s. Further up is Victory, site of the Battle of Bad Axe, which ended the Black Hawk War.

Genoa, seven miles north of Victory, was renamed in 1868 by Italian settlers, though the town little resembles its Mediterranean namesake. Just south is Lock and Dam Number 8, with an informa-

tive wayside park. About three miles north of Genoa, Old Settlers Overlook yields a breathtaking view of the river from atop a 500-foot bluff.

The road continues through the town of Stoddard, with a river beach at Stoddard Park, and by Goose Island County Park (608.785.9770), a recreational area on several islands. Five miles north is La Crosse, at the confluence of the La Crosse, Black, and Mississippi Rivers, considered one of Wisconsin's loveliest cities. Named by French settlers for a Winnebago Indian game, La Crosse is notable for its startling topography. (Buffalo Bill Cody found it so appealing that he bought part of Barron's Island.) For a taste of older days, catch a ride on a paddle wheeler, or visit the Italianate Hixon House (608.782.1980), preserved exactly as it was in the 1880s. Or take in the valley view (which looks on three states) from atop 600-foot-tall Grandad Bluff.

Wisconsin River Valley, near Prairie du Chien

WI 138 · WI 164

COVERED BRIDGE SCENIC BYWAY

| 48 miles | 2 hours | |

OHIO

Road Notes
The route traverses a pastoral corner of southeastern Ohio through Wayne National Forest, alternately snaking along the muddy Little Muskingum River and climbing onto steep, forested bluffs. Along the way are tiny towns, century-old covered bridges, and weathered barns. The drive is best from spring through fall; heavy snows may close the road in winter.

Start at Marietta (pg. 107, Q15)

Begin the drive at Marietta, site of the first permanent organized settlement in the Northwest Territory. After studying outpost history at the Campus Martius Museum (740.373.3750), a modern building that incorporates part of the original fort, head north on Route 26 through the city's outskirts.

About four miles ahead, the road twists along a wooded ridge overlooking hilly fields, deep hollows, and tree-covered highlands, then descends to the Little Muskingum valley floor. Along the river's floodplain are small corn and hay fields and some of the nation's oldest oil wells.

Detour a half mile east on Route 333 to Hills Covered Bridge. Built in 1878, it's one of more than 2,000 bridges – covered to protect the main structural timbers from inclement weather – that once spanned Ohio's rivers.

Back on Route 26, the Little Muskingum River soon appears on the right, in the shade of sycamores, box elders, and silver maples. The river's name is a Native American word meaning "muddy river." Popular in spring and fall with canoeists, the river lures anglers with more than 40 species of fish.

The drive continues along the river valley, rising occasionally to traverse bluffs and winding through small towns. Watch for Hune Covered Bridge, built in 1879. Cross it to hike a portion of the North Country National Scenic Trail, which one day will link New York and North Dakota.

After Route 26 leaves the river, beyond Rinard Mills, look for Knowlton Covered Bridge, built in 1887 and set in a tangle of wildflowers and native grasses. Three miles east on gravel Route 68 is Ring Mill, a historic house and former mill in use between 1846 and 1921, with a lovely riverside park. Back on Route 26, continue through hilly farm country. At the junction with Route 800, head north three miles to Woodsfield, a quiet little town at the end of the drive.

Buckeye Furnace Bridge

KENTUCKY HEARTLAND

| 30 miles | 1 hour | |

KENTUCKY

Road Notes
This rolling rural drive follows a former buffalo trace – a pathway regularly used by the great beasts, which were exterminated from this part of the country even before they vanished from the plains – and an early 19th-century Shaker toll road. The route then traverses Kentucky's famed bluegrass region and the rugged terrain of the Kentucky River Gorge.

Start at Lexington (pg. 63, G12)

Begin the drive in Lexington, home of the Kentucky Horse Park (800.568.8813), which features two museums and an array of annual equestrian events. Head south from downtown on South Broadway (U.S. 68). Soon after passing South Elkhorn Creek, urban development yields to modest plots of burley tobacco and lush pastures dotted with cows and hay bales.

The most prominent feature of this region is its miles of black-and-white fences, behind which thoroughbred horses graze in manicured meadows. This is the heart of Kentucky Bluegrass country, where the world's finest racing stock is bred. One of the most famous horse farms along the route is Almahurst Farm, ten miles outside of Lexington, which can be recognized by its cream-colored barns trimmed in forest green and burgundy. Beyond the farm, U.S. 68 winds past more horse farms, roadside stands, and weather-beaten tobacco barns.

Several miles after entering Jessamine County, the drive begins its descent into a narrow side valley of the Kentucky River Gorge. After 1.5 miles, the road crosses the Brooklyn Bridge, which spans the Kentucky River; from the bridge there's a fabulous view of the river's 300-foot-high limestone palisades. After several miles the land opens up into rough, rolling farmland.

Soon the buildings of the Shaker Village of Pleasant Hill (606.734.5411) appear. Although the colony effectively disbanded in 1910, many of the gray and pastel-colored Shaker buildings have been restored and are open for tours. Savor traditional Kentucky fare in the excellent dining hall of the Trustees Office.

The drive continues another seven miles, past more rolling pastureland, groves of walnut and oak trees, and antebellum mansions, before ending in Harrodsburg. Kentucky's oldest permanent settlement began as a fenced village in 1775, built to protect settlers from hostile Native Americans. A reproduction of the fort can be seen at Old Fort Harrod State Park (606.734.3314), near the original site.

From Harrodsburg, return to Lexington on U.S. 68 or take U.S. 127 to Danville, another fine old Kentucky town.

Bluegrass country, Lexington

NATCHEZ TRACE PARKWAY

| 270 miles | 1–2 days | 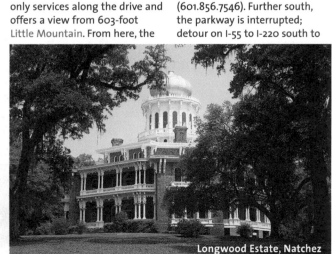 |

MISSISSIPPI

Road Notes
This two-lane parkway, administered by the National Park Service, parallels the original Natchez Trace – one of the United States' most famous frontier trails. From buffalo paths used by prehistoric hunters, the trace evolved into a series of Native American trails later trod by French and Spanish trappers, traders, missionaries, and soldiers – not to mention a few cutthroats and vagabonds. The parkway, in its entirety, stretches for 445 miles from Nashville, Tennessee, to Natchez, Mississippi. This drive begins at the Natchez Trace Parkway Visitor Center (mile 270) and goes south to Natchez (mile 0). Mileposts record mileages in reverse.

Start near Tupelo (pg. 80, C9)

Begin at the Natchez Trace Parkway Visitor Center (800.305.7417), which offers exhibits and an audiovisual presentation about the trace.

The Chickasaw Village (mile 261.8) marks the former Native American settlement and provides interpretations of Chickasaw life. The open country along this part of the drive, called the Black Belt for the color of its soil, is the remnant of a vast prairie. Enter an oak, hickory, and pine woods that is part of the Tombigbee National Forest (601.285.3264). Take a stretch under the fragrant pines at magical Witch Dance before heading south, past Bynum Mounds – remains of the prehistoric culture of the Mound Builders.

The next 40 miles offer a changing landscape of farms, pastureland, and forests. Jeff Busby Site (mile 193.1) has the only services along the drive and offers a view from 603-foot Little Mountain. From here, the trace soon crosses a bottomland of shrubs, which turns swampy for the next few miles, through Cole Creek and River Bend (mile 122.6). Just beyond, a boardwalk trail penetrates the eerie forest of bald cypress and tupelo at Cypress Swamp. The parkway follows the scenic Ross Barnett Reservoir for eight miles before reaching the Mississippi Crafts Center at Ridgeland (601.856.7546). Further south, the parkway is interrupted; detour on I-55 to I-220 south to I-20 west toward Vicksburg, then follow signs to rejoin the trace.

Mississippi's gracious capital, Jackson (601.960.1891), offers a walking tour of its historic downtown, which features stunning gardens and excellent museums.

Crossing Big Bayou Pierre four times, you get a view of its cultivated floodplain before reaching peaceful Mangum Site and Grindstone Ford. Now the parkway sweeps south past farms and wetlands, passing the Sunken Trace, a short trail along an eroded portion of the old trace, at mile 41.5. Here, the road begins to climb a ridge forested with hardwood and pine. The only inn remaining on the trace, Mount Locust (mile 15.5), built in 1810, is one of the oldest structures in the state. The parkway winds to its current southern terminus two miles farther on, when it intersects U.S. 61. Seven miles southwest lies Natchez (800.647.6724), an elegant vestige of the Old South containing a wealth of historic homes and estates.

Longwood Estate, Natchez

103 miles	4 hours	

FLORIDA

FLORIDA PANHANDLE SCENIC DRIVE

Road Notes

Lush vegetation, Old World architecture, dazzling white sand, emerald waters, and ultrakitsch await the visitor to Florida's Panhandle, which stretches 200 miles between Tallahassee and the Alabama border along the Gulf of Mexico. This drive hugs the Gulf shore from Pensacola to Panama City, meandering through live oak thickets and the ubiquitous tourist strips. Short of a hurricane, inclement weather is rare. The sun usually blazes, and a swimsuit is as much a necessity as a toothbrush.

Start at Pensacola (pg. 44, E3)

Begin the drive in Pensacola, site of the National Museum of Naval Aviation (800.327.5002), which has Skylab on display as well as an IMAX theater. The Pensacola Historical Museum (850.433.1559) has exhibits explaining why this city has flown five different flags. Bougainvillea-draped Seville Square Historic District, one of three, reflects a bit of the Old South's rural charm, and Historic Pensacola Village includes several fine buildings open to the public: The 1815 French Creole-style Lavalle House; Dorr House, a Greek Revival affair built in 1871; and the unpretentious Julee Cottage, owned by a free black woman in the early 1800s. In this historic district you'll also find a collection of oddities on the third floor of the T. T. Wentworth, Jr. Florida State Museum (850.595.5990), including stuffed Kodiak bears, a petrified cat, and a size 37 shoe.

Head east on Main Street (Bayfront Parkway / U.S. 98), past

Grayton Beach State Recreation Area

Pensacola Harbor and Pensacola Bay to where the road crosses three-mile-long Pensacola Bay Bridge heading out to Gulf Breeze. Here the road forks. You can continue east on U.S. 98 through the Naval Live Oaks Area, a trail-laced thicket of live oaks purchased in 1828 by the federal government to preserve the trees. The area is part of the 150-mile-long Gulf Islands National Seashore (850.934.2600). Another option is to pick up Route 399 and cross the Bob Sikes Bridge – watch for the much-loved '50s-era neon welcome sign – to Santa Rosa Island, a barrier island that is also part of the national seashore and offers unspoiled miles of live oaks, sea oats, and billowing sand dunes. The Blackbird Marsh Nature Trail passes through a teeming eco-system of exotic flora and fauna, including blue herons.

The two roads reconvene in the town of Navarre, the beginning of a stretch of hotels, amusement parks, and condominiums that continues to Panama City. Beyond the town of Fort Walton Beach, U.S. 98 returns to Santa Rosa Island and a recreation area on Choctawatchee Bay, which offers swimming and boating. The road cuts through a scenic stretch of pine-dotted dunes with Gulf vistas before crossing the mouth of the Choctawatchee Bay and

entering the town of Destin, immensely popular with charter-fishing enthusiasts.

Continue east through pine thickets and urban development; small side streets lead to lovely sandy beaches. Three miles east of Sandestin, detour onto Route 30A, a secondary road that angles 20 miles past lily-dotted lakes, pine thickets, and tiny towns. Highlights include Grayton Beach State Recreation Area (850.231.4210) and the resort village of Seaside.

About nine miles beyond Seaside, Route 30A joins U.S. 98 for the last brassy stretch to Panama City and its 27 miles of sandy beaches.

FL 44

FL 157

---

81 miles	2 hours	

GEORGIA

SEA ISLANDS

Road Notes

Georgia's shoreline is so interlaced with marshes, swamps, mudflats, and sloughs that no single coastal road can reveal all its beauty. The route that comes closest to the ideal is U.S. 17, which runs a few miles from the shore but winds through grassy tidal estuaries, pine thickets, and quaint shrimping villages. Traveling up the coast from Jekyll Island, this drive ends in Savannah, whose antebellum charm lingers in open squares, live oaks, and historic inns. Along the way, causeways and bridges branch off to a few of the state's "golden isles" – subtropical barrier islands where luxurious resorts jostle against salt marshes.

Start at Jekyll Island (pg. 49, P11)

Begin the drive at Jekyll Island, purchased in 1886 by 50 business magnates – among them Rockefellers, Pulitzers, and Vanderbilts – to be used as their exclusive winter playground. Their sumptuous homes are in the Jekyll Island Historic District (912.635.2119).

Take Jekyll Island Causeway (Route 520), pick up U.S. 17, and head north across the Brunswick River to Brunswick, founded in 1771 and one of Georgia's largest ports. To the north and east of Brunswick lie the green and fecund environs of the Marshes of Glynn. The ground teems with crabs, shrimps, oysters, fish, and alligators. A short boardwalk at the marshes' Overlook Park (junction of U.S. 17 and Route 25) provides a good vantage on marsh life.

Three of Georgia's barrier islands cluster together just east of Brunswick: Little St. Simons, accessible only by boat, and St. Simons and Sea Island, a quick jaunt across the F. J. Torras Causeway. Just before the cause-way is the Brunswick-Golden Isles Welcome Center (800.933.2627). At St. Simons Island, visit Fort Frederica National Monument (912.638.3639), an 18th-century town, now a scenic ruin. The hub of exclusive Sea Island is the Cloister (912.638.3611), a Mediterranean-style resort built in the 1920s.

Back on U.S. 17, continue for ten miles to Hofwyl-Broadfield Plantation State Historic Site (912.264.7333), dotted with camellias, magnolias, and ancient live oaks. Rice fields crossed with dikes and floodgates testify to the area's rich rice culture.

The drive continues across the flood delta of the Altamaha River, part of the 27,078-acre Altamaha State Waterfowl Management Area, a haven for herons, egrets, and other wading birds. On the river's north bank is Darien, founded in 1736 and renowned for its annual April blessing of the shrimp fleet. The road to the right, immediately after the Darien Welcome Center (912.437.6684),

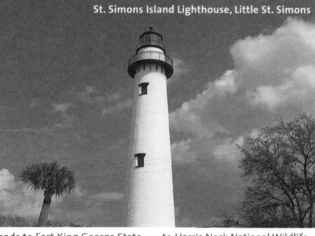
St. Simons Island Lighthouse, Little St. Simons

leads to Fort King George State Historic Site (912.437.4770), a reconstruction of the British Empire's southernmost continental North American outpost.

From Darien, continue on U.S. 17 through more coastal plain scenery. Or follow Route 99, a country road that passes Thicket, with its ruins of a sugar mill and a rum distillery. Route 99 rejoins U.S. 17 at Eulonia. Eight miles farther, detour seven miles east on Harris Neck Road to Harris Neck National Wildlife Refuge (912.652.4415), where as many as 30,000 wading birds congregate in late summer and fall. Back on U.S. 17, continue to the town of Midway and the Midway Museum (912.884.5837), filled with colonial furnishings and documents. The drive ends 30 miles farther, in Savannah, the embodiment of classic southern charm.

GA 48

GA 157

---

80 miles	2 hours	

MARYLAND

EASTERN SHORE

Road Notes

Separating the Chesapeake Bay and the Atlantic Ocean, the peninsula portion of Maryland is a land of broad tidal rivers, tranquil farmlands, and historic manors. Famous for its oysters, crabs, and clams, the Eastern Shore's shellfish abundance has in recent years been threatened with depletion, prompting government intervention. Consequently, it is now illegal to harvest oysters except from wooden boats called skipjacks – which explains why these rather antiquated vessels are still in use. The route begins in Chesapeake City and terminates at Dogwood Harbor on Tilghman Island, where the skipjack fleet docks.

Start at Chesapeake City (pg. 69, C17)

Chesapeake Bay

Begin the drive in Chesapeake City, a handsomely restored 19th-century town near the western end of the Chesapeake and Delaware Canal, built in 1829. The enormous waterwheel used through the early 1900s to regulate water levels is on view in the Old Lock Pump House (410.885.5621). The drive south along Route 213 passes by fields of corn and soybeans, two staples of the Delmarva (Delaware, Maryland, Virginia) Peninsula. Within the first 15 miles, the route crosses the Bohemia and Sassafras Rivers, which, during the 1700s, were indispensable thoroughfares for the great tobacco plantations of the area.

Continue to Chestertown, founded in 1706, with its stately Georgian and gaily painted Victorian homes, and some fine examples of pre-revolutionary architecture. Afternoon tea is served at the White Swan Tavern B&B (410.778.2300) on High Street. Just a mile past its intersection with U.S. 50, Route 213 ends at Wye Mills (410.827.6909), a 17th-century waterpowered gristmill. South of the mill, on Route 662, is 400-year-old Wye Oak, said to be the country's largest white oak tree.

Continue south on U.S. 50 toward Easton, where the 1684 Third Haven Friends Meeting House (410.822.0293) offers a glimpse of the town's Quaker heritage. Nearby, at the mouth of the Wye River, is Wye House (private), once the seat of a vast plantation where the abolitionist Frederick Douglass spent his boyhood as a slave. Near Easton, turn right onto Route 322, then right again onto Route 33 east and continue for 11 miles to St. Michaels, a charming harbor town with tidy inns, restaurants, and the excellent Chesapeake

Bay Maritime Museum (410.745.2916), dedicated to the history and workaday lore of the bay. The museum even has a lighthouse to explore.

Thirteen miles past St. Michaels, a tiny bridge leads over Knapps Narrows to Tilghman Island, home for centuries to hardy individuals who harvest the bay's bounty. Less than a half mile from the bridge, turn left on Dogwood Harbor Road to view Chesapeake Bay skipjacks, wooden sailing vessels ranging from 25 to 60 feet in length, which are usually docked here. The venerable craft are used in the local oyster industry.

At the fork, 2.5 miles farther on, bear right for a view of the bay along Black Walnut Point Road. The road ends in a half mile, at the gate of the Black Walnut Point Inn (410.886.2452), one of the most secluded B&Bs on the Eastern Shore.

MD 68

MD 159

FINGER LAKES DRIVE

| 39 miles | 1 hour | |

NEW YORK

NY 94

NY 161

Road Notes

Few topographical features are more aptly named than the Finger Lakes, which fan across the Allegheny Plateau like the outstretched digits of an enormous hand. This drive winds along the shoreline of the longest of them, 40-mile Cayuga Lake, where pleasant towns and fine wineries accent the countryside. Late spring through mid-fall the drive is best – wineries harvest at the end of summer.

Start at Ithaca (pg. 95, P13)

Begin in Ithaca, at the southern end of Cayuga Lake. As Route 89 heads north it first winds past Ithaca's outlying suburbs before cutting through Taughannock Falls State Park (607.387.6739), ten miles outside town. In addition to the falls, there are boat launches and rentals and a beach. At 215 feet, Taughannock is higher than Niagara, but there's no roaring cascade. The narrow white ribbon of water changes seasonally, needling down into a cold, green pool at the center of a vast natural amphitheater of shale.

Continue north past the falls, where Route 89 passes through tranquil lakeside farmland, with occasional views of Cayuga Lake and its eastern shore. The Finger Lakes region ranks as the largest wine-producing area in the East, and almost a dozen wineries are located just off the road here. In fact, this leg of Route 89 has been dubbed the Cayuga Wine Trail. Most of the wineries offer tours and on-site purchasing. Several roadside apiaries also sell honey.

For a pleasant side trip with outstanding lake views, turn right eight or nine miles north of Taughannock Falls onto Deerlick Springs Road, then left on Route 153, which winds through the small towns of Kidders and Sheldrake. Other than a few restaurants and B&Bs, the route is uncommercialized, passing gracious Victorian homes framed by big weeping willows whose branches drape out across the water. The shore road, now called Weyers Point Road, loops up and rejoins Route 89 after 4.5 miles, but the panoramas of the lake continue to the east. To the west, farmlands, orchards, and the occasional small town occupy the gently rising pillow of land that reaches across to the shores of Seneca Lake. Two of the rural communities here, Ovid and Romulus, typify the local penchant in the early 1800s for naming towns after people and places of classical antiquity.

The road hugs Cayuga Lake quite closely along much of the northern half of the route and ends in Seneca Falls, just west of Cayuga Lake on U. S. 20. Seneca Falls is home to several archives of women's history. Here, in the mid-19th century, Elizabeth Cady Stanton and Lucretia Mott laid the groundwork for the modern feminist movement by organizing the 1848 Women's Rights Convention in Declaration Park. The Elizabeth Cady Stanton House is preserved in the Women's Rights National Historical Park (315.568.2991). Exhibits at the National Women's Hall of Fame (315.568.8060) tell the stories of distinguished American women. And the Seneca Falls Historical Society (315.568.8412), a Queen Anne mansion, contains original documents of feminism's first wave.

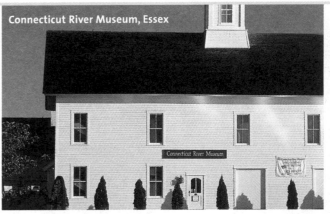
Taughannock Falls State Park

THE ADIRONDACKS

| 92 miles | 2½ hours | |

NEW YORK

NY 94

NY 161

Road Notes

A favorite retreat of mobsters and millionaires alike, the Adirondack Mountains are among the Northeast's last great wildernesses, with 42 peaks rising higher than 4,000 feet. At the heart of the region is the six-million-acre Adirondack Park, a harmonious blending of pristine lakes, dense forests, and picturesque villages. Turn-of-the-century industrialists built great camps as summer retreats on the shores of some of the more remote lakes. In fall, the foliage is magnificent. Roads can be extremely icy during winter storms, and visibility poor at higher elevations in snow and fog.

Start at Speculator (pg. 95, H20)

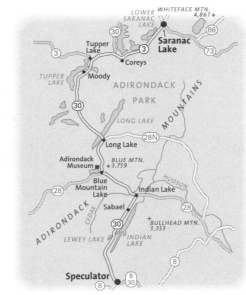

Begin at the intersection of Routes 8 and 30 in the village of Speculator, a hunting, fishing, and skiing center. Along Route 30 north, the mountains rise gradually and the forests of maple, beech, and birch explode with color in the fall. After 12 miles, just past Lewey Lake and the entrance to Lewey Lake Campground (518.457.2500), the road crosses a stream linking Lewey Lake with Indian Lake, which forms part of the Hudson River's headwaters. Following along the shore of Indian Lake, views of the distant peaks of the northern Adirondacks open up. After seven miles, a scenic turnoff takes in 3,353-foot Bullhead Mountain and surrounding peaks.

A mile past the turnoff, make a left at the T-junction in Indian Lake and continue on Route 30 across the Cedar River. Thirteen miles past Indian Lake is the small resort town of Blue Mountain Lake, home to a shop that sells the wooden slat chairs named for the region. Turn right and continue on Route 30. Ahead is the lake from which the town takes its name and, on the right, Blue Mountain itself. Its 3,759-foot summit is accessible by a 2.2-mile trail that begins about a mile north of town. Before the trailhead is the Adirondack Museum (518.352.7311), one of the country's finest regional museums, whose collection includes antique guideboats, furniture, and mementos of early resort life.

From the museum, the road descends through forests to Long Lake, which offers excellent trout fishing. Turn left at the town of Long Lake and continue on Route 30. After a 20-mile drive through the forest, follow Route 30/3 through the town of Tupper Lake, notable for its early 20th-century facades. As the road crests a hill on the east side of town, 4,867-foot Whiteface Mountain, one of the highest peaks in the Adirondacks, looms ahead.

Bear right onto Route 3 about five miles past Tupper Lake and follow a forested, mountainous road that opens onto spectacular views of Lower Saranac Lake. Just beyond is the town of Saranac Lake, where gingerbread cottages line the shore. Famous a century ago for its tuberculosis sanatorium, the town is now the largest community in the Adirondack Park and a hub for outdoor recreation. The drive ends at the intersection of Routes 3 and 86.

Town of Saranac Lake, Lower Saranac Lake

LOWER CONNECTICUT VALLEY

| 56 miles | 2 hours | |

CONNECTICUT

CT 40

CT 157

Road Notes

The towns and harbors along the lower reaches of the Connecticut River have hummed with activity for more than 300 years – but the valley still possesses many lovely undeveloped stretches. This drive explores the natural and human-made environments that inspired the Nature Conservancy to designate the tidelands of the Connecticut River one of the hemisphere's "last great places." The route is most scenic from May through October.

Start at Middletown (pg. 40, F10)

Begin in Middletown, home to Wesleyan University (860.685.2000), at the junction of Routes 9 and 66. Head east on Route 66 across the river into Portland, once a brownstone quarrying center. Five miles farther, in the village of Cobalt, turn right on Route 151 and head south for eight miles, then east on 149 to Moodus, where the 1816 Amasa Day House (860.873.8144) boasts federal and Empire furnishings.

Backtrack and head south on Route 149, to East Haddam, where musical performances and scheduled tours are offered at the Victorian Goodspeed Opera House (860.873.8668). From the junction of Routes 149 and 82 in East Haddam, head east on 82 to Route 156. Head south to the township of Old Lyme, once a vital shipbuilding hub and inspiration to painters of the American Barbizon school. South over the Connecticut River on I-95, take the first exit to Route 9, and the second exit off 9 to Route 154.

One mile north is Essex, settled in 1690. The first Connecticut warship, the Oliver Cromwell, was built here in 1775. Steamboat Dock, built in 1640 at the end of Main Street, is New England's oldest continuously operating wharf. Turn off onto Route 9 and follow signs past the 1776 Griswold Inn (860.767.1776), with its famed Tap Room, to the historic waterfront and the Connecticut River Museum (860.767.8269), home of a reproduction of the 1775 American Turtle, the first submarine.

North on Route 154, past the junction with Route 9, is the Essex Steam Train & Riverboat (860.767.0103). Further north, detour west on Route 148 for about five miles, then right on Cedar Lake Road to Pattaconk Reservoir and the 16,000-acre Cockaponset State Forest (860.345.8521), which boasts a number of New England's few tulip trees. Continue north on Route 154 to Haddam, and turn left at Walkley Hill Road to visit the 1794 Thankful Arnold House (860.345.2400), with its delightful vegetable and herb gardens. Return to Route 154 and continue north to Haddam Meadows State Park, a meadowland in the river's floodplain. The scenic portion of Route 154 ends some four miles ahead, at a pretty waterfall in Seven Falls State Highway Park. Just past the falls on the left, the stone slabs of Bible Rock are poised on edge like an open book. About a mile from the park is an entrance to Route 9 northwest back toward Middletown.

Connecticut River Museum, Essex

THE BERKSHIRES

120 miles	1 day	

MASSACHUSETTS

Road Notes

The Berkshire Hills of Massachusetts have long been a favorite rustic retreat – and the city dwellers who summer here have made them a major venue for art, music, and dance. This drive takes in Herman Melville's home and the Boston Symphony Orchestra, and joins Shaker simplicity with Gilded Age grandeur. The best (though busiest) times of year to tour the Berkshires are fall foliage season and summer; reserve accommodations well in advance if visiting during Tanglewood or other festivals.

Start at Williamstown (pg. 72, B2)

Start at Williamstown (413.458.9077), home to the Sterling and Francine Clark Art Institute (413.458.9545), renowned for its collection of paintings by American masters and French Impressionists. The Williams College Museum of Art (413.597.2429) highlights American art, while the Chapin Library of Rare Books, on the college grounds, contains Revolutionary War-era documents.

Head south on U.S. 7 and Massachusetts 43, along the Green River West Branch. Dipping into New York State, the route pushes south on New York 22 to U.S. 20. You're now in Shaker country. Mount Lebanon Shaker Village (518.794.9500) looks much as it did in the 19th century. Back over the border in Massachusetts, the fully restored Hancock Shaker Village (413.443.0188) is a testament to Shaker ingenuity.

Take Massachusetts 41/102/183 south to the Norman Rockwell Museum (413.298.4100). Tour guides, some of whom modeled for America's favorite illustrator

Congregation Church, Williamstown

as children, regale visitors with anecdotal tidbits. Down the road, turn onto Mohawk Lake Road for Chesterwood (413.298.3579), the summer home of sculptor Daniel Chester French. In the high-ceilinged studio, French labored over his greatest work, the Lincoln Memorial.

Backtrack to Massachusetts 102 and head east into Stockbridge (413.298.5200),

Rockwell's inspiration, and the setting for Arlo Guthrie's classic song, "Alice's Restaurant." Nearby is the shingle-style mansion Naumkeag (413.298.3239), designed by Stanford White. Its stunning gardens by Fletcher Steele were 30 years in the making.

Continue north on U.S. 7 toward Lenox, to the junction of Massachusetts 7A and The Mount (413.637.1899). Designed by novelist Edith Wharton, this turn-of-the-century mansion reflects the author's love of balance and symmetry. In the resort town of Lenox (413.637.3646), head out West Street (Massachusetts 183) to Tanglewood (413.637.1600), the summer home of the Boston Symphony Orchestra.

Further north on U.S. 7 is the turn for Arrowhead (413.442.1793), Herman Melville's home from 1850 to 1863. The classic *Moby Dick* was written in the upstairs room. Further north on U.S. 7, in Pittsfield (413.443.9186), the Herman Melville Memorial Room in the Berkshire Athenaeum (413.499.9486) contains a fine

collection of his personal memorabilia. The Berkshire Museum (413.443.7171) features paintings by American masters such as Albert Bierstadt.

At Lanesborough, turn right onto North Main Street for Mount Greylock State Reservation (413.499.4262) and the state's highest peak. An observation tower offers views of the Berkshire Valley and the Taconic Range. Descend Mount Greylock via scenic Notch Road, then take Massachusetts 2 east to Western Gateway Heritage State Park (413.663.8059). Here, an exhibit recounts the dramatic story of the nearby Hoosac Tunnel. Completed in 1875, the 25,000-foot engineering feat cost $20 million and almost 200 lives.

Return to Williamstown on Route 2, the "Mohawk Trail," which follows the trek made by Native Americans between the lush Connecticut and Hudson River Valleys.

MA 72
MA 159

WHITE MOUNTAINS SCENIC DRIVE

130 miles	½–1 day	

NEW HAMPSHIRE

Road Notes

New Hampshire's White Mountains, named for the white granite embedded in the hills, are the rooftop of New England and the centerpiece of the 800,000-acre White Mountain National Forest. Although most tourists (skiers excepted) explore this lofty realm in spring, summer, and fall, roads are generally well maintained throughout the year. Travel early in the day – and on weekdays in summer – to avoid heavy traffic that can slow down driving on popular routes such as the Kancamagus Highway. Weekends in fall foliage season attract a lot of traffic to the mountains, and winter is a season of famously unpredictable weather.

Start near Littleton (pg. 89, F6)

Start at the junction of U.S. 302 and I-93, just south of Littleton. At Franconia, a narrow dirt road leads to the battered mailbox marking The Frost Place (603.823.5510), a simple white farmhouse where poet Robert Frost once lived. It's now a museum with first editions and Frost memorabilia.

South of town, I-93 merges with the nearly nine-mile-long Franconia Notch Parkway, cutting through Franconia Notch. On a clear day you can look far into Vermont and Maine from the top of 4,100-foot Cannon Mountain. An aerial tramway (603.823.5563) is the quickest way to the summit. The New England Ski

Frost Place, Franconia

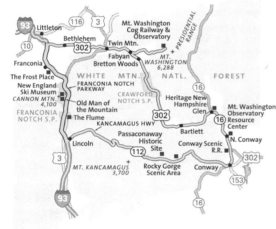

Museum (603.823.7177), at the base of the mountain, traces the sport's history. Farther south, stop at Profile Lake for a great view of the natural stone formation known as the Old Man of the Mountain. Just ahead lies the Flume, a 180-million-year-old natural gorge whose granite walls rise up to 90 feet.

Just outside Lincoln, pick up the Kancamagus Highway, a National Forest Scenic Byway that meanders east for 37 miles through pristine wilderness and climbs to nearly 3,000 feet as

it traverses the flank of Mount Kancamagus. The Swift River forms natural pools at the Rocky Gorge Scenic Area, a popular swimming spot.

Turn north on Route 16 to North Conway and check the weather conditions atop Mount Washington at the Mount Washington Observatory Resource Center (603.356.2137). Just north of the Route 16–U.S. 302 junction in Glen, Heritage New Hampshire (603.383.9776) reviews the state's history from 1634 to the present.

The six-mile stretch of U.S. 302 through Crawford Notch State Park offers spectacular views of the Presidential Range. In Bretton Woods, just beyond Crawford Notch, is the 1902 Mount Washington Hotel (800.258.0330). Modeled after a luxury cruise ship, it's the largest wooden building in New England.

With its rack rails and valiant little cog-driven locomotives, the nearby Mount Washington Cog Railway (800.922.8825) has been hauling passengers to the 6,288-foot summit since 1869. Only three miles long, the railway is also one of the steepest. Up top, you can visit Mount Washington Observatory museum, and on a clear day you can see forever – all the way to the ocean at Portland, Maine.

At the turn of the century, the pure air of Bethlehem (603.869.2151), farther west on U.S 302, made the town a popular destination for hay fever sufferers. The main street is lined with old hotels. Continue west on U.S. 302 to return to I-93.

NH 89
NH 161

ROUTE 100

100 miles	½ day	

VERMONT

Road Notes

Route 100 is the Main Street of Vermont's Green Mountains, running alongside the state's rugged spine from Massachusetts almost to Québec. This drive covers one of the most scenic portions of the route, terminating in Smugglers' Notch, where peregrine falcons nest beneath rugged thousand-foot cliffs. The drive is most scenic from late spring through mid-fall, with fall foliage peaking earlier in the north. Traffic can be heavy in high summer and foliage season.

Start at Weston (pg. 130, J4)

Begin in Weston, considered one of Vermont's prettiest villages and home to Weston Playhouse (802.824.5288) and the Vermont Country Store (802.824.3184). Bear right 3.5 miles north of Weston and follow Route 100 for seven hilly miles into Ludlow, a former mill town turned into a lively agglomeration of shops and restaurants.

Continue on Route 100 back into rural Vermont. On the right, Lake Rescue soon comes

into view, followed by Echo and Amherst Lakes – all strung together by the Black River. Continue for three miles, past the northern end of Amherst Lake and detour onto Route 100A for a two-mile side trip into tiny Plymouth Notch, where Calvin Coolidge became president. The hamlet's houses, barns, and old Coolidge-family store are now part of the President Calvin Coolidge State Historic Site (802.672.3773).

Return to Route 100 and continue north along the Black River Valley, reaching U.S. 4 at West Bridgewater. The Ottauquechee River here once turned the wheels of Bridgewater's woolen mills. Route 100 and U.S. 4 merge along the river, climbing in elevation as they pass the Killington Ski Area (802.422.3333), which spans two mountains.

When the routes diverge, bear right on Route 100, which enters a wooded stretch of mountainous terrain, with the northern section of the Green Mountain National Forest on the left. Continue north to Rochester, one of the loveliest towns along this stretch. The route passes through the steep-sided White River Valley to the Granville Reservation. Look to the left for lovely Moss Glen Falls, cascading down a sheer rock wall 1.4 miles into the reservation. Continue for three miles, to Route 100 and the Mad River Valley – more ski country.

In Irasville, detour left onto Route 17 to the Sugarbush and Mad River Glen Ski Areas. The

12-mile stretch of Route 100 between Waitsfield and Waterbury is largely farmland with fine mountain views.

Just a mile past the point where Route 100 crosses I-89 is one of Vermont's most popular attractions, Ben & Jerry's Ice Cream Factory (802.244.8687). Three miles beyond, at the Cold Hollow Cider Mill (802.244.8771), visitors can watch cider being made. Ten miles north of Waterbury is Stowe, a town long synonymous with skiing and the famous Trapp Family Lodge (802.253.8511). The tiny town is clustered around the 1833 Green Mountain Inn (802.253.7301). In the center of town, Route 108 leads to Mount Mansfield – at 4,393 feet, the highest point in Vermont and a skiing center, with Stowe Mountain Resort and Smugglers Notch Ski Area. Smugglers Notch is a scenic natural pass that saw considerable action during Prohibition. Backtrack to I-89 to continue east or west.

VT 130
VT 164

Stowe

CAPE BRETON

Road Notes
The finest scenic drive in Canada's maritime provinces winds around Cape Breton's northern shores overlooking the Gulf of St. Lawrence, and climbs into the moody highlands of Cape Breton National Park – one of Canada's most magnificent wilderness areas. The route then follows the Atlantic coast to South Gut St. Ann's, site of North America's only Gaelic college.

Start at Baddeck (pg. 153, H14)

Begin the drive in Baddeck, the adopted home of Alexander Graham Bell, one of the founders of the National Geographic Society. The Alexander Graham Bell National Historic Site (902.295.2069) presents an exciting, interactive walk through his world, and houses the most complete collection of his memorabilia, artifacts, and equipment. Drive a few miles west on Trans-Canada 105 to join the famous Cabot Trail – named for explorer John Cabot. Then head north to North East Margaree through the narrow wooded valley of the Middle River, a favorite among salmon and trout anglers. After about 32 kilometers, stop by the Margaree Salmon Museum (902.248.2848), housed in an old schoolhouse.

As the route winds north along the river valley to the coast, the landscape becomes more rugged, remote, and barren, and the communities become smaller and more scattered. Up the hill, in St. Joseph du Moine, stop by the whimsical Gallery La Bella Mona Lisa (902.224.2560), a fine collection of provincial folk art. At Chéticamp, gateway to the highlands, the landmark St. Peter's Church (1893) was built of stone from Chéticamp Island. The Acadian Museum (902.224.2170) features the local cottage industry – hooked rugs.

The moody highlands loom ahead at the entrance to Cape Breton Highlands National Park (902.224.2306, 902.285.2691), the rugged roof of Nova Scotia. To take advantage of pulloffs, detours, and serendipitous diversions, allow at least five hours for this 106-kilometer park drive. Among the highlights: The towering walls of Chéticamp Canyon, MacKenzie Mountain look-off, the ascent up 475-meter North Mountain (watch for moose), and the fishing villages and narrow, isolated beaches along the Atlantic coast. Drive on to the Ingonish area. Just outside town, Cape Smokey Lodge (902.285.2778) operates a chairlift up a 300-meter vertical slope to the top of Old Smokey Mountain. Continue south along the coast for about 80 kilometers to South Gut St. Ann's, settled by Highland Scots. The Gaelic College of Celtic Arts and Crafts (902.295.3411) has exhibits on Scottish history and culture and offers demonstrations of traditional weaving, music, and dance. The craft shop stocks nearly 300 tartans. Continue south on the Cabot Trail to return to Baddeck.

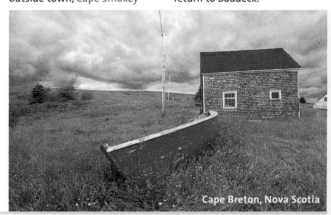
Cape Breton, Nova Scotia

EASTERN TOWNSHIPS

Road Notes
This drive begins in Montréal, the world's second largest French-speaking city, then heads through pastoral Montérégie into the region called either Cantons-de-l'Est, by French-speaking Quebecois, or the Eastern Townships, by Anglophones, of which there are several significant pockets – reflecting early 19th-century British settlement – in this part of Québec. Along the way, the route passes through picturesque wine country.

Start at Montréal (pg. 151, L12)

Begin in Montréal (800.363.7777), located on an island in the St. Lawrence River. The cosmopolitan city, founded by France as a missionary colony in 1642, retains a decidedly French flair. Adjacent to the hilltop Parc du Mont-Royal, designed by Frederick Law Olmsted, is the huge copper-domed Oratoire Saint-Joseph (514.733.8211), a popular religious shrine. The Biodôme de Montréal (514.868.3000), a unique environmental museum, re-creates four distinct ecosystems.

Head east on Route 10 across Pont Champlain. Exit at Chambly and continue through town to historic Chambly Canal, where keepers manually operate the old locks. Fort Chambly National Historic Site (450.658.1585) preserves the site of a 1665 French stockade, replaced in 1709 by a stone fortification. Proceed south on Route 223 through the Richelieu Valley. Just beyond Saint-Paul-de-l'Île-aux-Noix is the British fortification at Fort Lennox National Historic Site (450.291.5700). A ferry transports visitors to l'Île-aux-Noix, the small island on which the fort stands.

Head south on Route 223 to pick up Route 202 east, la Route des Vignobles (the "vintners trail"), which traverses rolling wine country. Lac Champlain comes into view near the modest summer resort of Venise-en-Québec. The road winds around the lake's north shore before veering northeast into the Eastern Townships (800.355.5755). Look south for a breathtaking view of New York's Adirondack Mountains and Vermont.

To the east lies the heart of wine country, Dunham, a quaint village blessed with a microclimate that produces excellent apples and grapes. Take Routes 202, 104, 243, and 245 to Bolton Centre, detouring toward Austin and following the signs to the Abbaye de Saint-Benoît-du-Lac (819.843.4080), situated above Lac Memphrémagog. Several times daily, monks at the Benedictine abbey recite prayers in Gregorian chant.

Head north to Magog via Chemin Nicholas-Austin and take Route 112 east to Sherbrooke (800.561.8331), the regional capital of the Eastern Townships. In the Magog River Gorge, Centrale Frontenac (819.821.5406), Québec's oldest operating hydroelectric plant, offers interactive exhibits, guided tours, and the interpretive Magog River Trail. Head west on Route 112. In Deauville, continue west to return to Magog (800.267.2744) at the head of Lac Memphrémagog, a pristine 48-kilometer-long body of water that extends south between wooded shores into Vermont. Continue on Route 112 through Waterloo, on the Yamaska River, which sprang to prominence with the arrival of the railway. A part of the original line has been converted into Estriade Cycle Path, providing bikers with a scenic link to Granby's Lake Boivin. In Granby, the Granby Zoo (877.472.6290) is home to some one thousand animals of 225 different species. The Centre d'Interprétation de la Nature du Lac Boivin (450.375.3861) provides some of the best bird-watching vantage points in Québec. Return to Montréal via Route 112 or Route 10, a limited-access expressway.

Place Jacques Cartier, Montréal

THE ROUTE TO KLONDIKE GOLD

 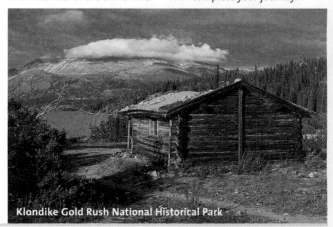
Road Notes
As resonant a part of frontier history as any event, the 1897–98 Klondike gold rush brought tens of thousands of prospectors into a ferociously wild, hard land by way of one of two 33-mile-long, brutally steep foot trails and a float trip of some 500 miles up the Yukon River. This drive follows the first part of the stampeders' journey toward the goldfields. Beginning in the former boomtown port of Skagway, in Alaska, the drive climbs over White Pass on a highway that roughly parallels the trail the sourdoughs used, then stops near Whitehorse, the capital of the Yukon Territory. Finally, the route heads west to the Kluane Lake area, arguably the most spectacular part of the 1,400-mile Alaska Highway.

Start at Skagway (pg. 24, F10)

Once a major gateway for the Klondike gold rush, Skagway (907.983.2855) lies at the mouth of a slender canyon. Brush up on gold rush history at the Visitor Center for the Klondike Gold Rush National Historical Park (907.983.2921).

Follow Highway 2 north out of Skagway. Soon, you climb out of the gorge and top 3,292-foot White Pass, where you'll descend into the gentler landscape of this part of the Yukon interior, with its immense lakes. Whitehorse (867.667.7545) sprang to life as a gold rush transportation hub connecting Dawson City and Skagway.

Downtown, along the startling blue waters of the Yukon River, is the S.S. Klondike National Historic Site (867.667.3910), where a guided tour of the gleaming 1930s paddle wheeler offers riverboat lore. Near the airport is the Yukon Transportation Museum (867.668.4792), with a time line of the region's history. Heading west from Whitehorse, the Alaska Highway glides over the southern fringe of the Yukon Plateau. For thousands of years, this region has been home to the Southern Tutchone people – Athapaskans who had no direct contact with Europeans until the mid-19th century. Stop at the Long Ago People's Place (867.667.6375), just east of Champagne, where you can learn how the Tutchone tanned hides, dried fish, and hunted with ingenious traps and tools. Beyond Champagne lie the jaw-dropping ramparts of the Kluane Ranges. This abrupt line of glaciated peaks stands above a sprawling valley and extends along the entire eastern front of Kluane National Park Reserve (867.634.7207). Hidden behind this imposing wall lies the heart of the park – an intensely wild landscape with one of the world's largest nonpolar ice fields, the St. Elias Mountains. In Haines Junction, stop at the park's excellent Visitor Reception Centre. To the north is 40-mile-long Kluane Lake. North across the mudflats of the Slims River Delta is the Sheep Mountain Visitor Centre, dedicated to Dall sheep, Kluane's most abundant large mammal. From here, the Alaska Highway continues on to Alaska, where you can follow the highway to its terminus in Fairbanks or take the Tok cutoff to Anchorage. If you want to return to Skagway, return to Haines Junction and follow the Haines Highway to Haines, where a ride on an Alaska Marine Highway ferry (800.642.0066) will complete your journey.

Klondike Gold Rush National Historical Park

70 miles | 3 hours

BAJA'S GOLD COAST

Road Notes

Northern Baja's craggy coastline is home to a strange hybridized culture of Moorish castles, tiny fishing villages, and luxury resort developments. Once you've crossed the border from San Ysidro, the road curves around the *playas*, or beaches, of Tijuana, past the grand "Bullring-by-the-Sea." If you take the toll road (Mexico 1-D), the modern highway hugs the coast of the Mexican Riviera, a booming stretch of high-rise hotels, condominiums, and golf courses. Tolls are collected at three points for a total of about six dollars. The free two-lane road (Mexico 1) winds through a mountainous area for 16 kilometers before crossing the toll road at Rosarito. Both roads follow the coast for the next 50 kilometers before the free road turns inland again at La Misión. Mexico 1-D is dotted with kilometer markers from Tijuana (K0) to Ensenada (K112).

Start at Tijuana (pg. 154, A1)

MEXICO HIGHWAY 1 SOUTH

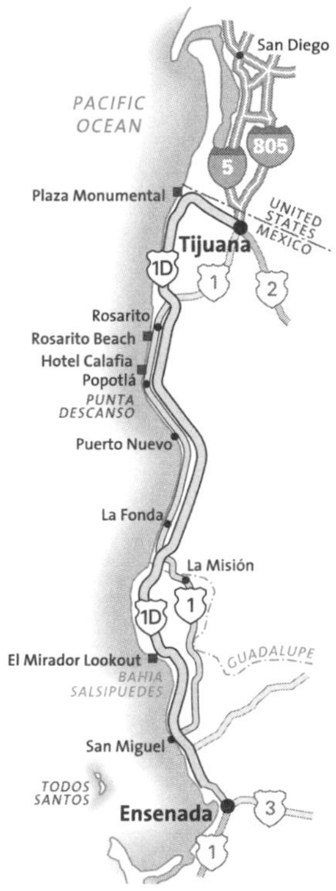

Tijuana (66.852.197) is the second largest city along the Pacific Coast after Los Angeles. For a quick visit, focus on Avenida Revolución, the city's main drag. Hucksters beckon you to look at their cheap leather sandals outside stores selling Luis Vuitton luggage. At the southern end of the street is the landmark Frontón Palacio – the jai alai stadium. From Avenida Revolución, follow signs for Carretera Cuota (a toll road) to avoid having to navigate through downtown Tijuana.

Mexico 1-D, the toll highway, climbs out of the smoky valley that encloses Tijuana and skirts a residential area along the city's beaches. The most visible sight is the Plaza Monumental, ten kilometers west of town, which is the second largest bullring in the world. Bullfights run from May through September. South of the border, at kilometer 29 (K29), is Rosarito Beach (800.962.2252), a popular resort destination. In the center of town is the Rosarito Beach Hotel (661.2.0144), once frequented by Hollywood stars like Lana Turner, Mickey Rooney, and Rita Hayworth. A dozen other hotels and condominiums are perched on cliffs above the huge, white-sand beach.

From Rosarito, you can continue south on either the toll road or the free road since they follow essentially the same route. The toll road is less congested and gives you better views of the coast, but there are only a few places to pull over. About ten kilometers south of Rosarito Beach is the Hotel Calafia, a sprawling resort perched on cliffs high above the beach. The ocean-view restaurant is a great place for whale watching. The Spanish galleon perched on an outside deck is a bar and nightclub.

As you continue south, look for the Puerto Nuevo exit sign at about K44. This tiny seaside town with the dirt roads is Baja's lobster capital, with more than

Matador, cape men, and bull, Tijuana

20 restaurants, all specializing in Puerto Nuevo-style lobster, where the *langosta* is lightly fried in oil before being briefly grilled.

Just past La Fonda, at K65, the free road turns inland again and weaves its way through mountains before joining Mexico 1-D just north of Ensenada at San Miguel. The toll road continues to hug the coast. Stop at El Mirador Lookout, at K84, for dramatic views of tranquil Bahia Salsipuedes and the glittering shoreline that is often referred to as Baja's Big Sur. If it's a clear day, you'll spot two craggy outcroppings some 20 kilometers offshore. This is Isla de Todos Santos, a popular spot for both anglers and surfers. From here it's another 25 kilometers to the bustling port city of Ensenada, known for its seafood taco stands and tourist bars, including the landmark Hussong's Cantina (61.78.3210), which has been selling cold *cerveza* since 1892.

50 miles | 6 hours

MAUI

Road Notes

Known as one of Hawaii's most scenic routes, the Hana Highway winds along the coast past waterfalls and rocky streams, through rain forests, and among tropical blossoms and fruit trees. The twisting "highway," built in 1927 by convict laborers, is well paved but narrow, with around 600 curves and many stops while oncoming traffic crosses one-lane bridges. Set out early in the day, pull over for restless drivers behind you, and take it easy. It's the trip that counts here, not the destination.

Start at Kahului (pg. 50, E8)

HANA HIGHWAY

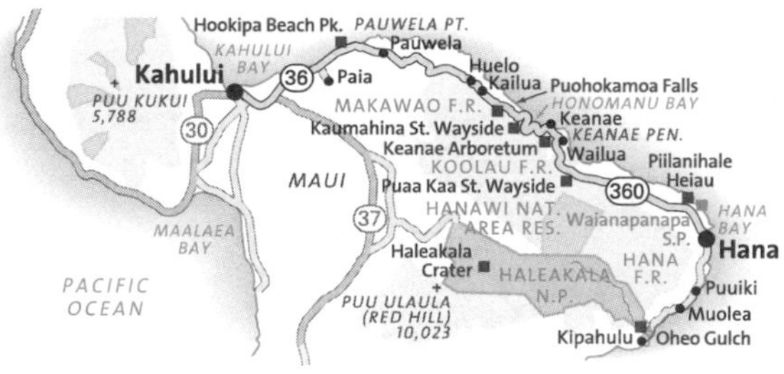

Route 36 begins in Kahului. A surf-laced coastline and sugarcane fields appear alongside you on the seven miles to Paia, the last place before Hana to fill your gas tank and picnic basket. Paia is a laid-back colony of hippies, craftspeople, and windsurfers, who show their stuff at Hookipa Beach Park, near the nine-mile marker past town.

Just past the 16-mile marker, the road is renumbered at Route 360, and mile markers go back to zero. This is the start of the "real" Hana Highway. Gardens and mailboxes sprout up when you reach tiny Kailua, where many residents work on the ditches that carry rainwater from the wet uplands to the dry cane fields of central Maui. Along this stretch, guava trees and mountain apples are common.

Past the nine-mile marker, stop at the short Waikamoi Ridge Trail to stroll among tall eucalyptus trees, their trunks twined with South American taro vines. On the road just ahead are Waikamoi Falls and Puohokamoa Falls, the latter a fine picnic spot with pools to swim in. Then continue just over a mile to Kaumahina State Wayside Park and its expansive view over the coastline.

The road runs along several hundred feet above the sea, then skirts U-shaped Honomanu Bay (entrance just past the 14-mile marker). After you climb the bay's far side, there is a small pullout with a stunning view back over the bay.

In about two miles you reach the Keanae Arboretum, where trails lead to native and introduced plants (taro, breadfruit, banana, bamboo, ti, and ginger). Just ahead is the road down to the Keanae Peninsula, an extension of land created by lava that spilled down from Haleakala, the dormant volcano that dominates eastern Maui. Down in quiet Keanae village, whose residents are mainly native Hawaiians, there is a restored 1860 stone church and cultivated patches of taro, the source of poi. You can get a good view of the peninsula from the small, unmarked Keanae Overlook, just past the 17-mile marker.

Now comes a stretch where the road climbs high above the ocean. Above this region, Haleakala's slopes receive an average of 390 inches (and sometimes as much as 500 inches) of rain yearly, which accounts for the many waterfalls through here. One of the prettiest is

Waterfall on Haleakala

beyond the 22-mile marker at the wayside park of Puaa Kaa.

Stop at Waianapanapa State Park, which offers a black-sand beach and caves formed of collapsed lava tubes. The water inside sometimes turns red – some say because of clouds of small shrimp, while others cite the legend of a slain Hawaiian princess whose blood tinges the water.

Within a few miles you reach the pastoral town of Hana, which is quiet and unspectacular, though its setting between Hana Bay and the green hills is lovely and its mood timeless. The main businesses are ranching and the upscale Hotel Hana-Maui (808.248.8211), started in 1946. Do see the Hawaiian artifacts and crafts on display at the Hana Cultural Center (808.248.8622) and visit the 1838 Wananalua Church, built of lava rock.

165 miles | 1–3 days

PUERTO RICO

Road Notes

The best known of the island's rural routes connects Yabucoa in the southeast with Mayagüez on the west coast, passing through the Cordillera Central, Puerto Rico's mountainous backbone. From the east, the route climbs quickly into the hills, often reaching heights of more than 900 meters. Ahead, a network of roads provides views of magnificent tropical scenery and glimpses of traditional rural lifestyles. The verdant terrain – a refuge for hundreds of bird species – includes *flamboyan*, *yagrumo*, and mango trees, bamboo, sierra palms, and giant luminescent tree ferns. One-day trips are recommended at right. A good map, with the route highlighted, is essential. Plant and bird guidebooks are also useful.

Start at Yabucoa (pg. 156, B5)

RUTA PANORÁMICA

Day 1: From Yabucoa to Cayey. The loop around Yabucoa and Maunabo – coastal towns where camping on the beach is permitted – offers lovely views of the ocean and sugarcane fields. The route then ascends into the Sierra de Cayey and bisects the Carite Forest Reserve, which borders a lake of the same name. The 6,000-acre state forest, just an hour from San Juan, is the natural habitat of 50 species of birds, including the Puerto Rico tanager, a brilliantly colored songbird, as well as the golden *coquí*, a native Puerto Rican tree frog. Waterfalls and intensely blue pools, like the small Charco Azul, are scattered throughout the forest.

Day 2: From Cayey to Adjuntas. The spectacular San Cristóbal Canyon, wedged between the towns of Aibonito (the highest town on the island) and Barranquitas, was formed by volcanic processes during Puerto Rico's rise from the ocean floor. A scenic overlook at Degetau Rock provides magnificent views of valleys and mountains, bursting with flowers and tropical growth. In Barranquitas, visit the Muñoz Mausoleum and Muñoz Rivera Library Museum (787.857.0230), which memorialize the island's 19th-century patriot Luís Muñoz Rivera.

Continuing on toward Adjuntes, the highest lake on the island, Guineo Reservoir, and the tallest peak, 4,390-foot Cerro de Punta, sit in the lush Toro Negro State Forest. The scenery here is a blend of stunning mountain terrain, that overlooks both the Atlantic and the Caribbean, and junglelike forests of sierra palms. Detour on Route 140 to reach the town of Jayuya, on the northern border of Toro Negro, which is noted for its skilled and meticulous wood-carvers.

Day 3: From Adjuntas to Mayagüez. Former coffee estates and coffee groves surround the town of Adjuntas, a leading producer of *cintrón*. West of Adjuntas the route crosses the dam of Lake Garzas and ascends to remote Guilarte State Forest, where woodpeckers, cuckoos, and hawks nest in mahogany, *tabanuco*, and trumpet trees. A short, often slippery trail leads to the summit of Monte Guilarte. Beyond are several villages in the heart of coffee country.

The Maricao Fish Hatchery (787.838.3710), in the town of Maricao, raises some 25,000 fish each year to stock farm fishponds and island lakes. The hatchery, set in tropical gardens, is part of the Maricao State Forest, home to numerous bird species. A stone observation tower reveals long vistas of the western coast and the Mona Passage, which separates Puerto Rico from the rest of the Greater Antilles. Finish the route at Mayagüez, Puerto Rico's third largest city.

Sierra de Cayey

MEX 154
MEX 165
HI 50
HI 158
PR 156
PR 165

	ANNISTON	AUBURN	BIRMINGHAM	CHATTANOOGA TN	COLUMBUS GA	DECATUR	DEMOPOLIS	DOTHAN	FLORENCE	GADSDEN	HAMILTON	HUNTSVILLE	MERIDIAN MS	MOBILE	MONTGOMERY	OPP	SELMA	TUSCALOOSA
BIRMINGHAM	66	141		149	167	83	92	191	121	63	92	101	258	88	166	94	61	
DOTHAN	207	125	191	311	97	273	198		310	251	282	291	246	199	103	66	147	237
HUNTSVILLE	100	241	101	109	266	25	215	291	65	74	104		245	357	187	265	194	156
MOBILE	279	227	258	403	252	340	144	199	377	317	286	357	132		173	146	194	205
MONTGOMERY	106	54	88	234	79	170	100	103	207	148	179	187	153	173		81	51	134

DRIVING DISTANCES IN MILES

SEE ALSO MILEAGE AND DRIVING TIME MAP ON PAGES 6–7

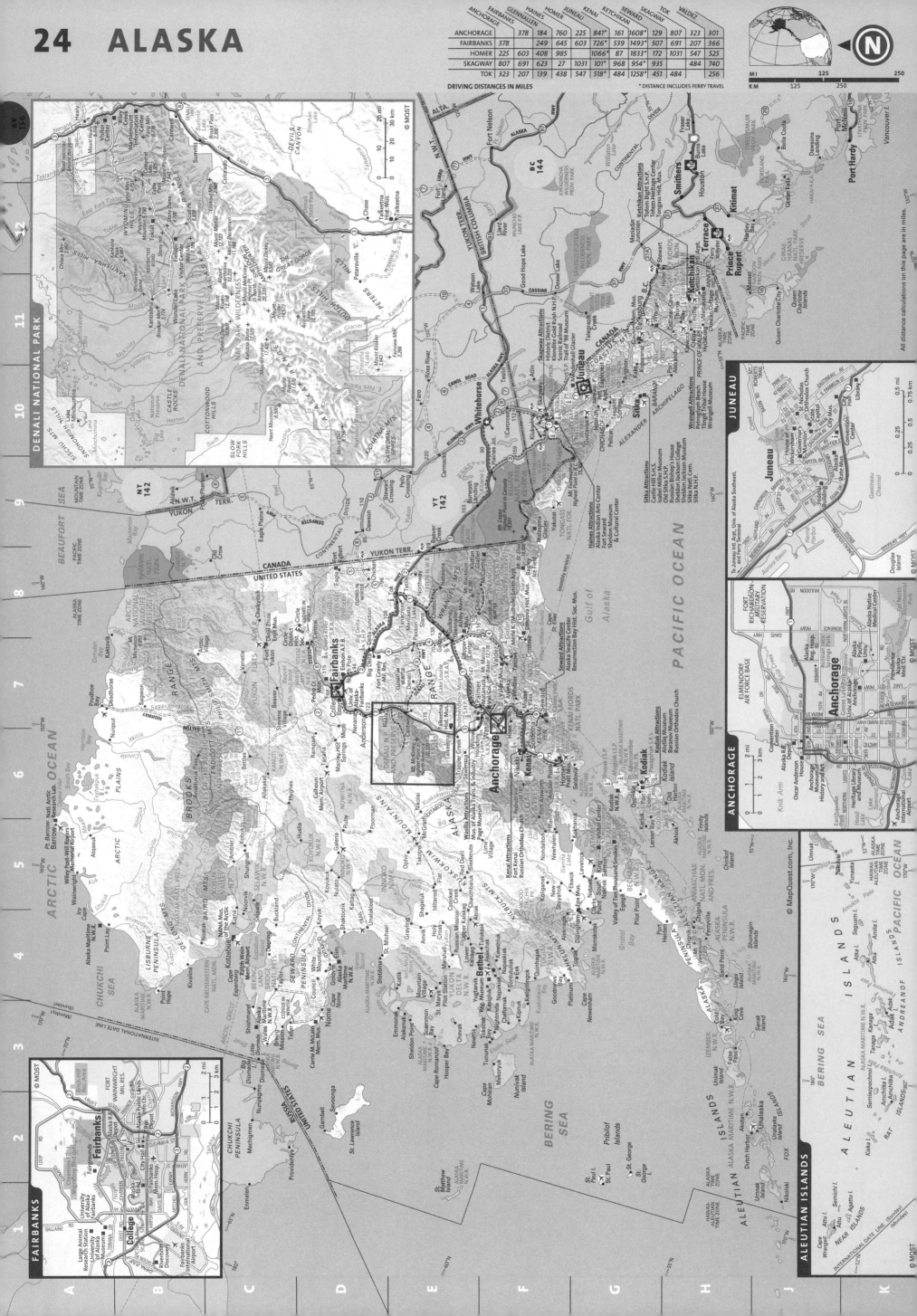

	ANCHORAGE	FAIRBANKS	HAINES	HOMER	JUNEAU	KENAI	KETCHIKAN	SEWARD	SKAGWAY	TOK	VALDEZ
ANCHORAGE		378	184	760	225	841*	161	1608*	129	807	323	301
FAIRBANKS	378		249	645	603	726*	539	1493*	507	691	207	366
HOMER	225	603	408	985		1066*	87	1833*	172	1031	547	525
SKAGWAY	807	691	623	27	1031	101*	968	954*	935		484	740
TOK	323	207	139	438	547	518*	484	1258*	451	484		256

DRIVING DISTANCES IN MILES   * DISTANCE INCLUDES FERRY TRAVEL

All distance calculations on this page are approximate.

DENALI NATIONAL PARK

FAIRBANKS

ANCHORAGE

JUNEAU

ALEUTIAN ISLANDS

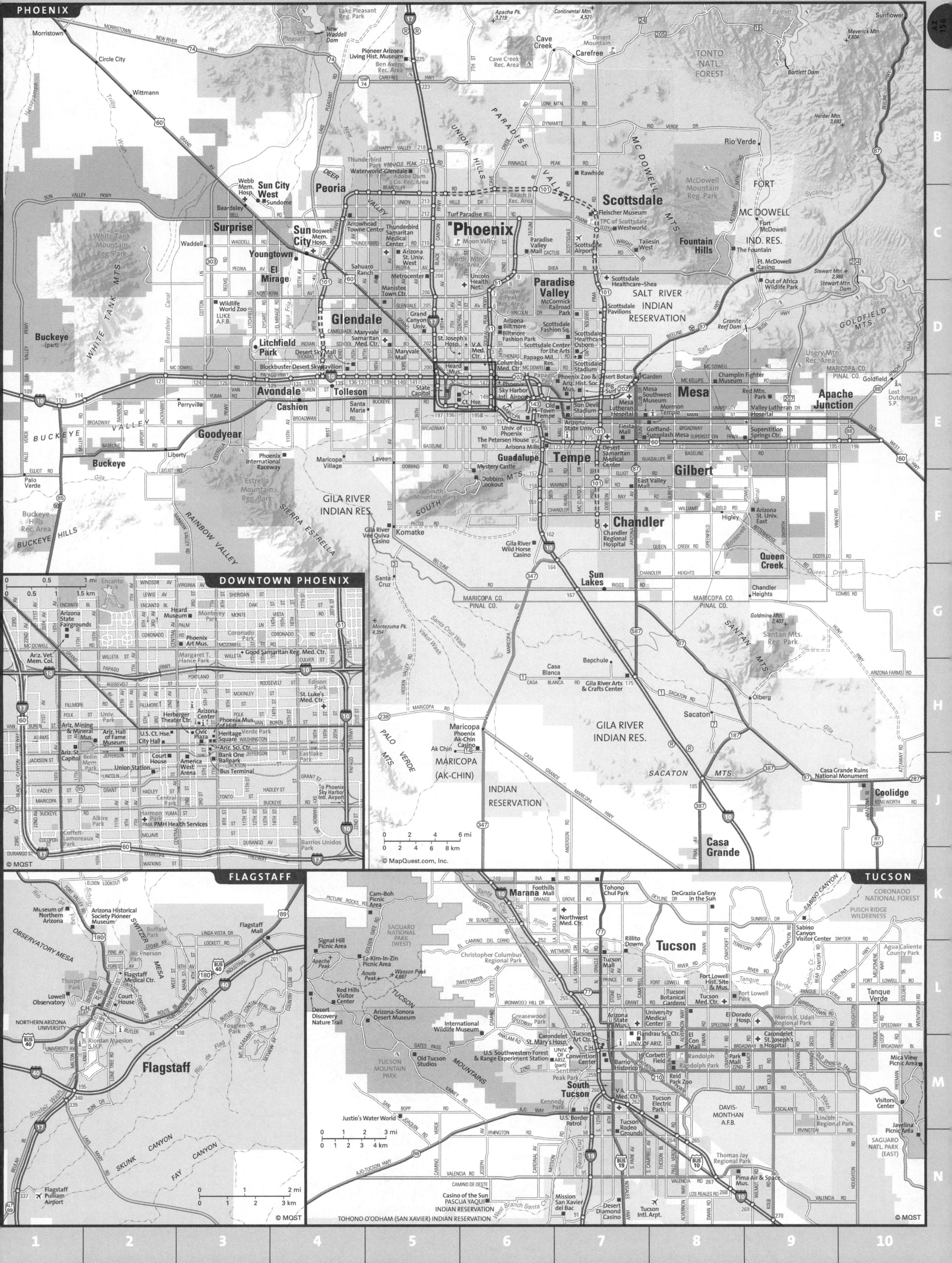
PHOENIX
DOWNTOWN PHOENIX
FLAGSTAFF
TUCSON
Phoenix
Scottsdale
Glendale
Peoria
Mesa
Tempe
Gilbert
Chandler
Surprise
Sun City West
Sun City
Avondale
Goodyear
Buckeye
Litchfield Park
Paradise Valley
Fountain Hills
Apache Junction
Queen Creek
Sun Lakes
Casa Grande
Coolidge
GILA RIVER INDIAN RES.
SALT RIVER INDIAN RESERVATION
TONTO NATL. FOREST
Flagstaff
Tucson
South Tucson
Marana
Tanque Verde
DAVIS-MONTHAN A.F.B.
© MapQuest.com, Inc.
© MQST

MI 25 50
KM 25 50

N

UTAH | COLORADO | NEW MEXICO
NEVADA | CALIFORNIA

Major cities and places:

Las Vegas, N. Las Vegas, Henderson, Boulder City, Laughlin, Needles, Bullhead City, Kingman, Lake Havasu City, Parker, Blythe, Quartzsite, Ehrenberg

Phoenix, Mesa, Tempe, Chandler, Gilbert, Scottsdale, Glendale, Peoria, Sun City, Surprise, Avondale, Buckeye, Goodyear, Fountain Hills, Carefree, Cave Creek, Apache Junction, Queen Creek, Wickenburg

Flagstaff, Williams, Sedona, Cottonwood, Camp Verde, Prescott, Prescott Valley, Chino Valley, Payson, Globe, Superior

Page, Tuba City, Kayenta, Chinle, Window Rock, Gallup, Zuni Pueblo, St. Johns, Eagar, Springerville, Show Low, Pinetop-Lakeside, Snowflake, Taylor, Holbrook, Winslow

Kanab, Fredonia, Colorado City, Hurricane, Washington, St. George, Hildale, Littlefield, Mesquite, Overton

Grand Canyon, Grand Canyon National Park, Kaibab Nat. For., Coconino Nat. For., Prescott Nat. For., Tonto Nat. For., Apache Nat. For., Sitgreaves Nat. For.

Navajo Indian Reservation, Hopi Ind. Res., Fort Apache Ind. Res., San Carlos Ind. Res., Hualapai Ind. Res., Havasupai Ind. Res.

Painted Desert, Monument Valley, Vermilion Cliffs, Echo Cliffs, Mogollon Plateau, Coconino Plateau, Kaibab Plateau, Shivwits Plateau

PACIFIC TIME ZONE | MOUNTAIN TIME ZONE

DRIVING DISTANCES IN MILES

	BULLHEAD CITY	CASA GRANDE	CHINLE	DOUGLAS	FLAGSTAFF	GRAND CANYON	HOLBROOK	KINGMAN	LAKE HAVASU CITY	NOGALES	PAGE	PHOENIX	PRESCOTT	SAFFORD	SHOW LOW	TUCSON	WICKENBURG	YUMA
FLAGSTAFF	180	188	216	374		89	93	148	209	318	135	137	89	271	140	255	147	215
KINGMAN	34	235	364	421	148	175	240		60	365	281	184	150	353	288	302	134	215
PHOENIX	217	50	353	237	137	226	230	184	193	181	272		96	169	178	118	51	183
TUCSON	335	68	366	120	255	345	240	302	311	65	390	114	214	128	193		169	241
YUMA	222	179	536	360	320	409	413	215	155	304	455	181	213	368	352	241	170	

SEE ALSO MILEAGE AND DRIVING TIME MAP ON PAGES 6–7

	BLYTHEVILLE	CAMDEN	CONWAY	DUMAS	EL DORADO	FAYETTEVILLE	FORT SMITH	HARRISON	HELENA	HOT SPRINGS	JONESBORO	LITTLE ROCK	MEMPHIS, TN	MENA	NEWPORT	PINE BLUFF	RUSSELLVILLE	TEXARKANA
FORT SMITH	353	201	134	255	232	64		141	280	126	266	165	266	95	298	81	220	210	87	180
JONESBORO	53	236	133	185	253	287	266		178	111	200		135	70	276	46	180	182	49
LITTLE ROCK	195	101	31	90	118	186	165	136	122	65	135		140	141	89	45	81	110
PINE BLUFF	213	76	76	45	93	231	210	181	106	76	180	45	157	151	134		126	128
TEXARKANA	99	210	104	129	227	259	238	193	62	174	49	110	49	250	53	128	154	

DRIVING DISTANCES IN MILES

SEE ALSO MILEAGE AND DRIVING TIME MAP ON PAGES 6–7

JONESBORO

PINE BLUFF

LITTLE ROCK

© MQST

DOWNTOWN SAN FRANCISCO

DOWNTOWN DENVER

ROCKY MOUNTAIN NATIONAL PARK

DENVER

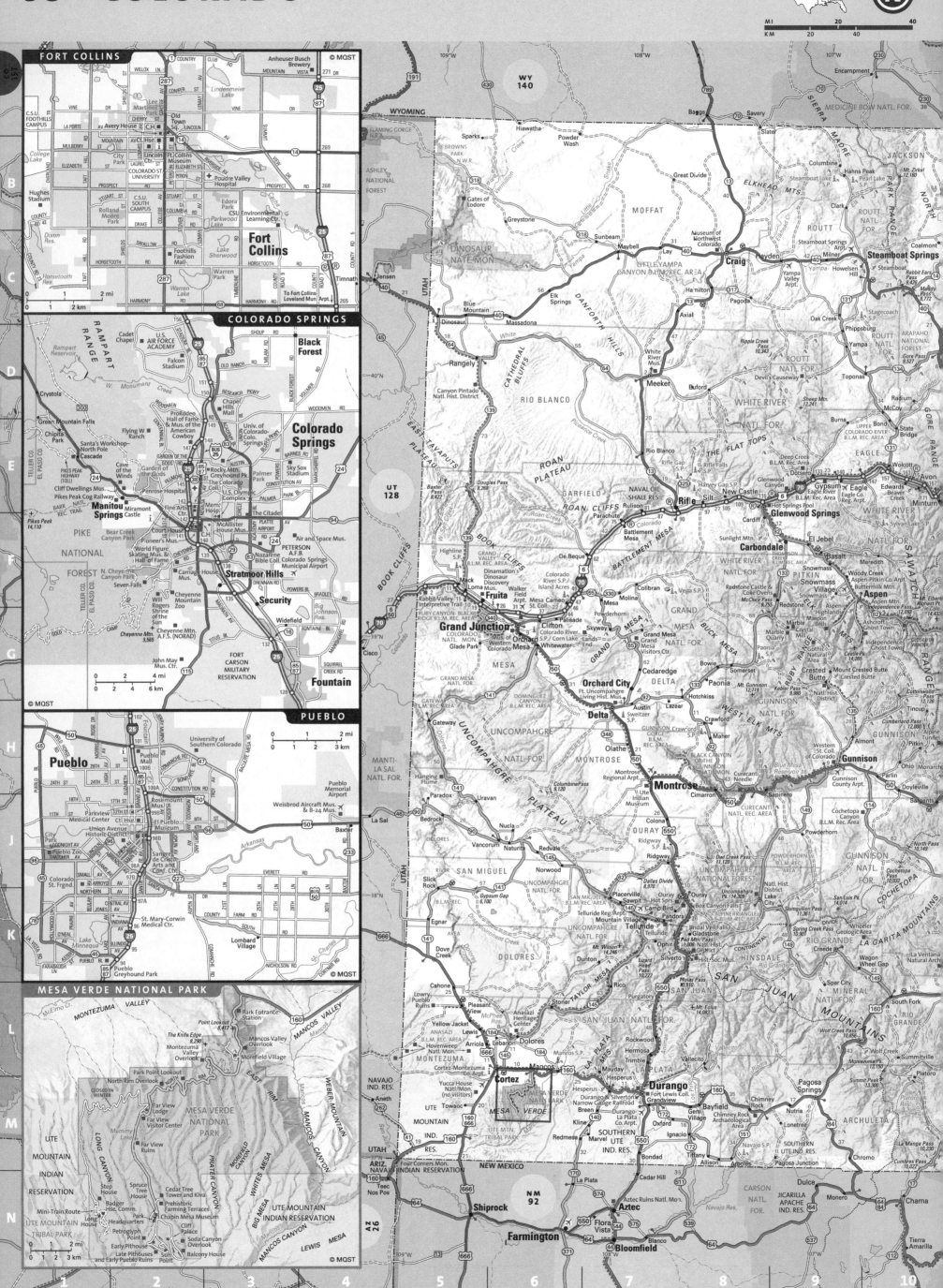

	ALAMOSA	ASPEN	BOULDER	BURLINGTON	COLORADO SPRINGS	CRAIG	DENVER	DURANGO	ESTES PARK	FORT COLLINS	GLENWOOD SPRINGS	GRAND JUNCTION	GREELEY	LAMAR	MONTROSE	PUEBLO	STERLING	TRINIDAD
COLORADO SPRINGS	162	157	97	152		270	70	314	133	226	318	133	161	236	43	194	127
DENVER	230	164	27	168	70	203		337	64	64	158	250	64	208	277	111	130	196
DURANGO	152	244	366	461	314	321	337		402	399	226	169	399	354	107	271	465	260
GRAND JUNCTION	261	135	254	418	318	152	250	169	291	311	92		311	458	62	360	377	444
PUEBLO	119	185	139	191	43	312	111	271	175	175	268	360	175	118	229		236	84

DRIVING DISTANCES IN MILES

SEE ALSO MILEAGE AND DRIVING TIME MAP ON PAGES 6–7

11   12   13   14   15   16   17   18   19   20

© MapQuest.com, Inc.

42 DELAWARE

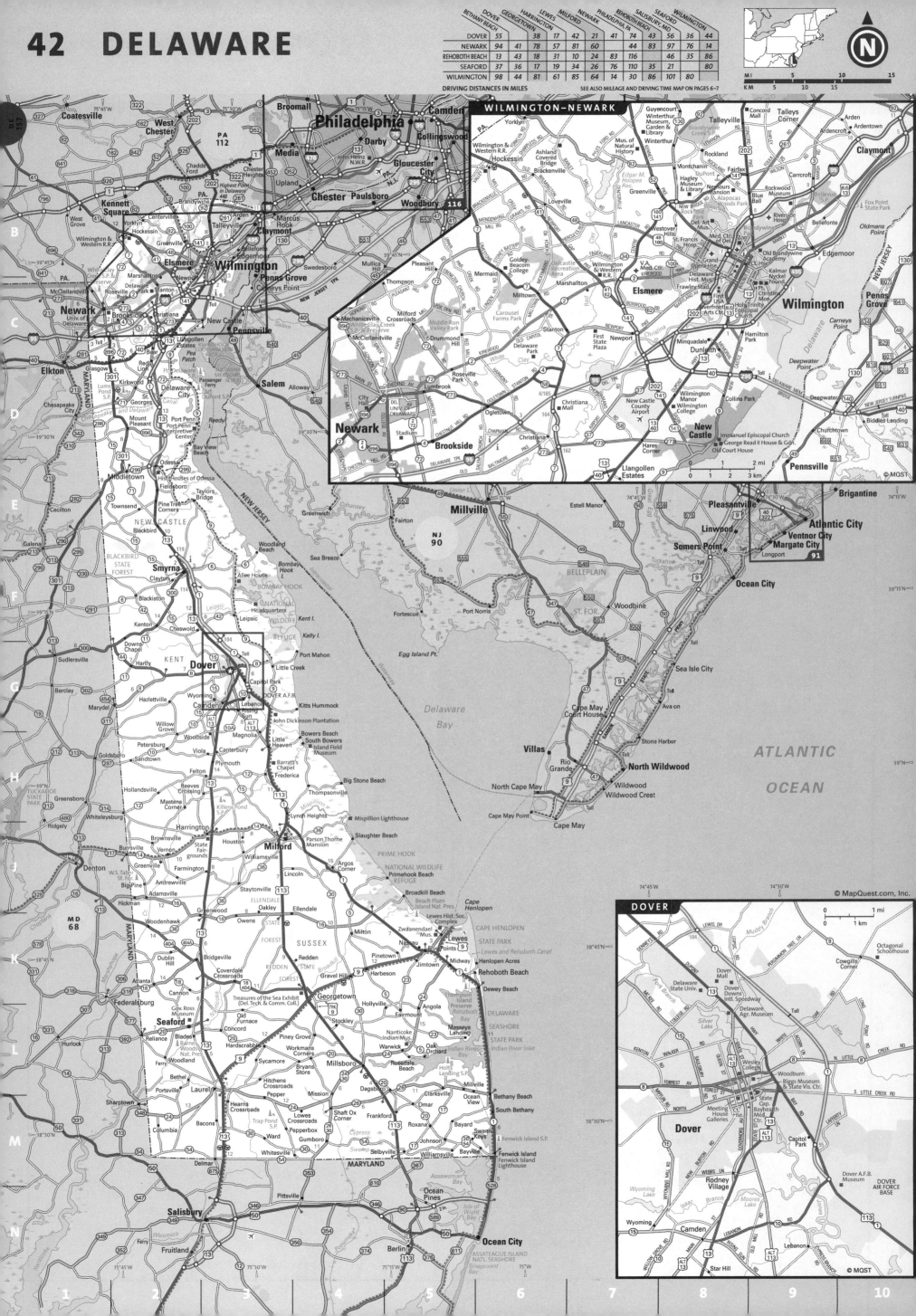

	DOVER BETHANY BEACH	GEORGETOWN	HARRINGTON	LEWES	MILFORD	NEWARK	PHILADELPHIA, PA	REHOBOTH BEACH	SALISBURY, MD	SEAFORD	WILMINGTON
DOVER	55	38	17	42	21	41	74	43	56	36	44
NEWARK	94	41	78	57	81	60		44	83	97	76	14
REHOBOTH BEACH	13	43	18	31	10	24	83	116		46	35	86
SEAFORD	37	36	17	19	34	26	76	110	35		21	80
WILMINGTON	98	44	81	61	85	64	14	30	86	101	80	

DRIVING DISTANCES IN MILES   SEE ALSO MILEAGE AND DRIVING TIME MAP ON PAGES 6-7

© MapQuest.com, Inc.

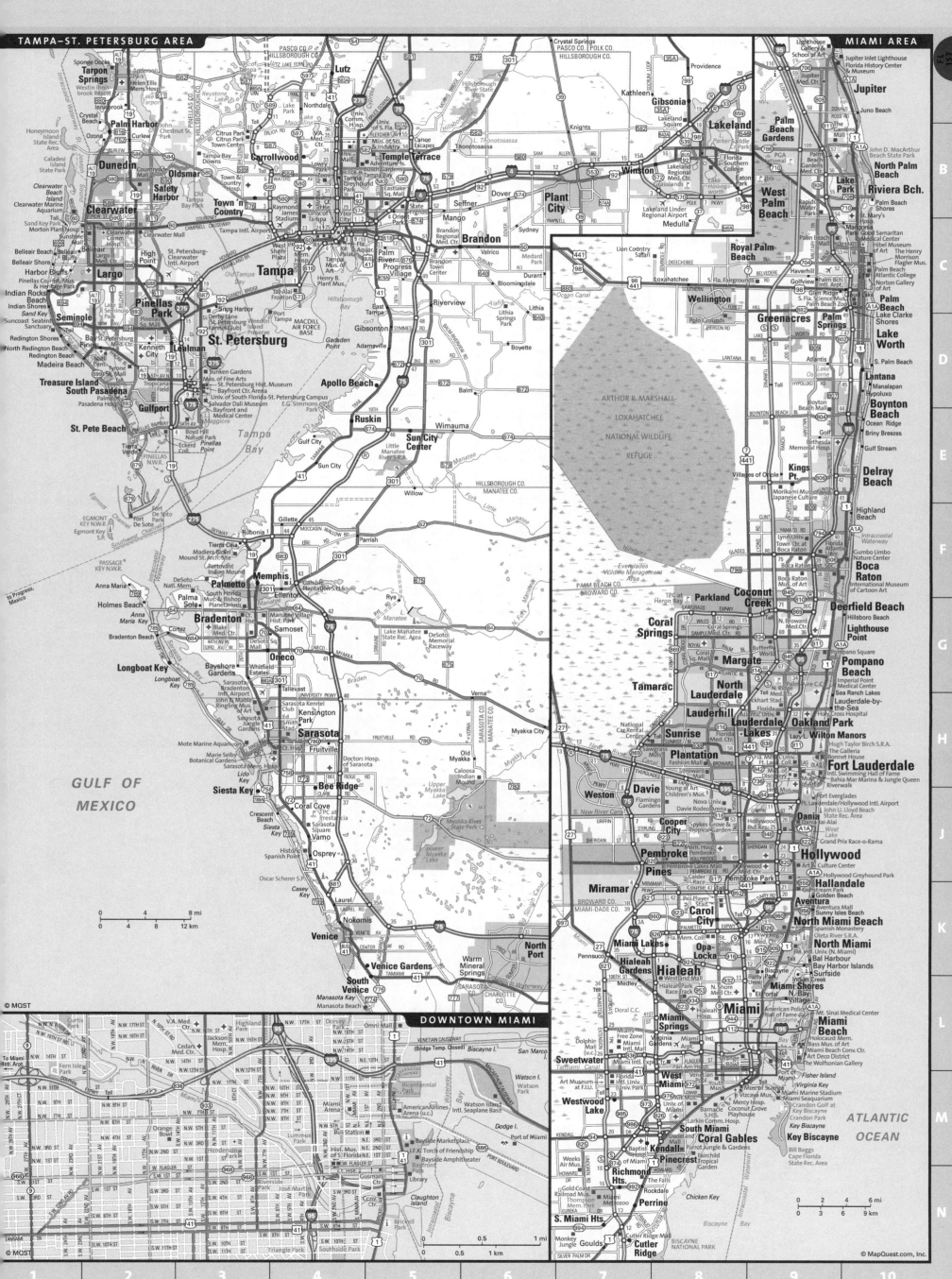

GULF OF MEXICO

ATLANTIC OCEAN

DOWNTOWN MIAMI

© MapQuest.com, Inc.

MI 20 40
KM 20 40

PENSACOLA — **PANAMA CITY** — **TALLAHASSEE**

(Inset maps)

Pensacola area: Ensley, Ferry Pass, Brent, Bellview, West Pensacola, Myrtle Grove, Brownsville, Pensacola, Warrington, Gulf Breeze, Univ. of W. Fla., Pensacola Reg. Arpt., Pensacola Naval Air Station, Old Pensacola Lighthouse, Gulf Islands Natl. Seashore, Fort Pickens, Perdido Bay, Escambia Bay, Santa Rosa Sound, Pensacola Bay

Panama City area: Lynn Haven, Hiland Park, Panama City, Springfield, Cedar Grove, Bayview, Magnolia Beach, St. Andrews Bay, West Bay, North Bay, Tyndall A.F.B., Bay Medical Center, Panama City-Bay County Intl. Airport

Tallahassee area: Tallahassee, Tallahassee Mall, Tallahassee Community Hosp., Florida State Univ., Florida A&M Univ., Mus. of Florida History, Doak Campbell Stadium, Tallahassee Regional Airport, Lake Jackson, Lake Lafayette, Lake Munson

---

ALABAMA / GEORGIA / FLORIDA (main map)

Mobile, Bay Minette, Spanish Fort, Daphne, Fairhope, Point Clear, Saraland, Creola, Atmore, Flomaton, Century, Jay, Walnut Hill, McDavid, Cantonment, Gonzalez, Pace, Milton, Bagdad, Harold, Holt, Crestview, De Funiak Springs, Argyle, Ponce de Leon, Westville, Caryville, Bonifay, Chipley, Cottondale, Marianna, Grand Ridge, Sneads, Chattahoochee, Gretna, Quincy, Havana, Midway, Tallahassee, Chaires, Woodville, Crawfordville, Sopchoppy, Panacea, St. Teresa, Carrabelle, Lanark Village, Apalachicola, Eastpoint, St. George Island

Bainbridge, Cairo, Climax, Donalsonville, Blakely, Cuthbert, Georgia

Pensacola, Gulf Breeze, Navarre, Milton, Niceville, Valparaiso, Shalimar, Fort Walton Beach, Destin, Mary Esther, Eglin A.F.B., Freeport, Santa Rosa Beach, Seagrove Beach, Grayton Beach, Panama City, Panama City Beach, Lynn Haven, Springfield, Callaway, Parker, Mexico Beach, Port St. Joe, Apalachicola

GULF OF MEXICO

Highest point in Florida 345

St. Vincent I., St. Vincent N.W.R., St. Joseph Peninsula S.P., Cape San Blas, Dog Island

---

ORLANDO — **JACKSONVILLE**

Orlando area: Apopka, South Apopka, Forest City, Altamonte Springs, Casselberry, Winter Springs, Fern Park, Maitland, Lockhart, Fairview Shores, Winter Park, Eatonville, Ocoee, Pine Hills, Winter Garden, Orlovista, Orlando, Azalea Park, Union Park, Conway, Pine Castle, Belle Isle, Sky Lake, Edgewood, Bay Hill, Doctor Phillips, Tangelo Park, Williamsburg, Buena Ventura Lakes, Kissimmee, Celebration, Walt Disney World, Magic Kingdom, Epcot Center, Disney-MGM Studios, Disney's Animal Kingdom, Lake Buena Vista, SeaWorld Orlando, Universal Studios Florida, Orlando International Airport, Lake Apopka

Jacksonville area: Jacksonville, Jacksonville International Airport, Orange Park, Bellair, Fernandina Beach, Amelia Island, American Beach, Yulee, O'Neil, Nassau Village, Atlantic Beach, Neptune Beach, Jacksonville Beach, Ponte Vedra Beach, Palm Valley, Sawgrass, Mayport Naval Station, St. Johns River, Big Talbot Island S.P., Little Talbot Island S.P., ATLANTIC OCEAN

© MQST

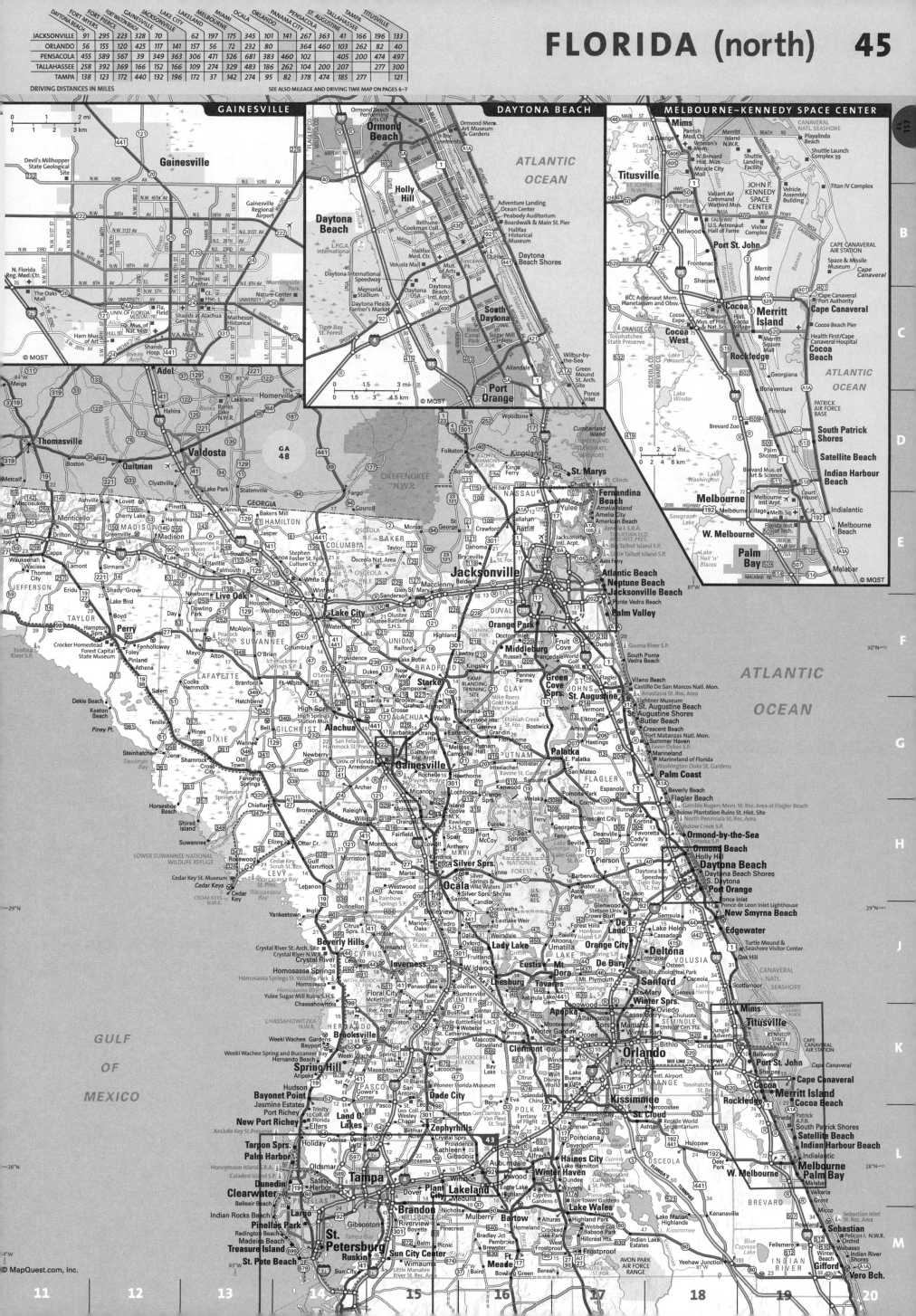

	ALBANY	AMERICUS	ATHENS	ATLANTA	AUGUSTA	BAINBRIDGE	BRUNSWICK	CHATTANOOGA TN	COLUMBUS	DUBLIN	GAINESVILLE	LA GRANGE	MACON	ROME	SAVANNAH	STATESBORO	VALDOSTA	WAYCROSS
ATLANTA	180	129	70		149	236	308	113	106	139	55	69	84	66	249	211	228	253
AUGUSTA	226	206	97	149		282	194	266	249	95	136	212	123	219	135	81	274	184
MACON	102	83	89	84	123	159	225	201	95	55	142	114		154	165	127	151	159
SAVANNAH	246	226	225	249	135	248	78	366	244	114	307	279	165	319		53	168	106
VALDOSTA	90	119	239	228	274	80	120	346	183	100	287	226	151	298	168	173		62

DRIVING DISTANCES IN MILES

SEE ALSO MILEAGE AND DRIVING TIME MAP ON PAGES 6–7

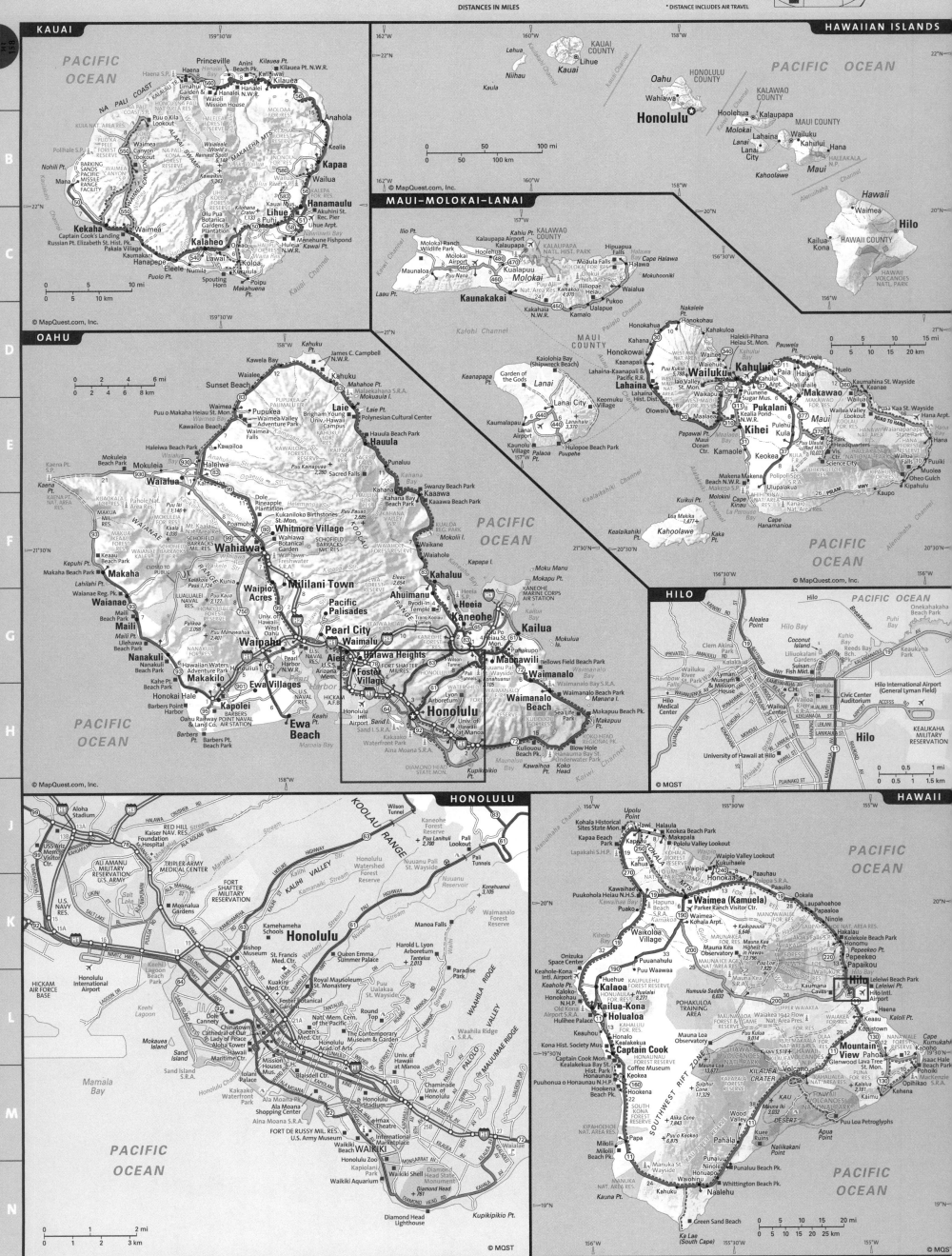

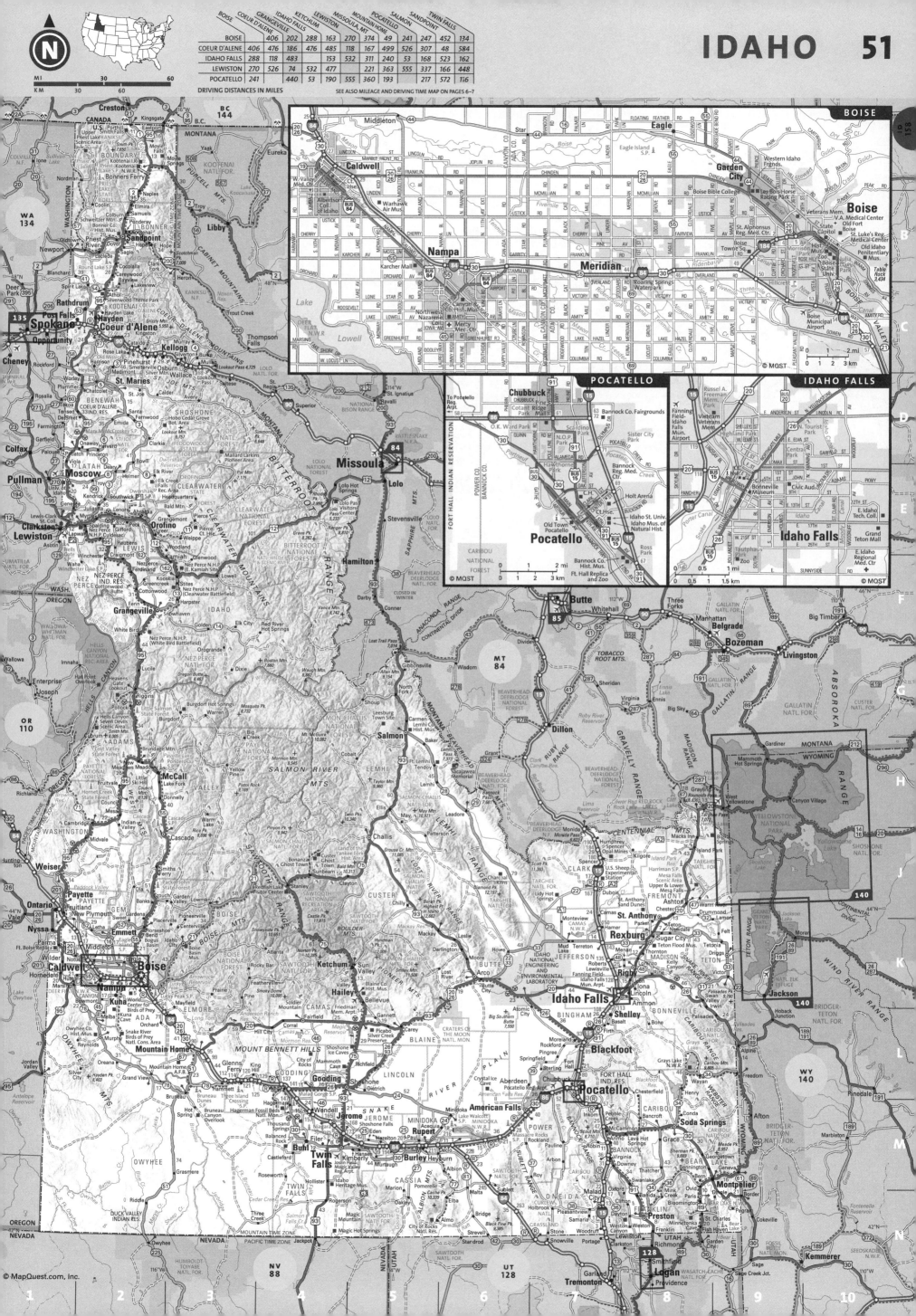

	BOISE	COEUR D'ALENE	GRANGEVILLE	IDAHO FALLS	KETCHUM	LEWISTON	MISSOULA, MT	MOUNTAIN HOME	POCATELLO	SALMON	SANDPOINT	TWIN FALLS
BOISE		406	202	288	163	270	374	49	241	247	452	134
COEUR D'ALENE	406		476	186	476	485	118	167	499	526	307	48	584
IDAHO FALLS	288	118		483		153	532	311	240	53	168	523	162
LEWISTON	270	526	74	532	477		221	363	555	337	166	448
POCATELLO	241		440	53	190	555	360	193		217	572	116

	CAIRO	CARBONDALE	CHAMPAIGN	CHICAGO	DECATUR	DUBUQUE, IA	EFFINGHAM	GALESBURG	JOLIET	KANKAKEE	MOUNT VERNON	PEORIA	QUINCY	ROCK ISLAND	ST. LOUIS, MO	SPRINGFIELD	
	BLOOMINGTON																
CHAMPAIGN	54	241	199		141	52	263	77	141	115	94	197	189	191	179	87
CHICAGO	135	376	334	141		186	180	212	198	40	61	280	168	306	86	169	294	197
ROCKFORD	134	424	382	189	86		184	93	260	153	99	139	328	135	272		124	293	196
ST. LOUIS, MO	160	156	105	179	294	116	342	103	220	257	252	81	172	131	293	270		97
SPRINGFIELD	63	254	182	87	197	40	245	89	123	160	152	158	75	110	196	173	97	

DRIVING DISTANCES IN MILES   SEE ALSO MILEAGE AND DRIVING TIME MAP ON PAGES 6–7

QUAD CITIES

CHAMPAIGN-URBANA

SPRINGFIELD

Champaign

Davenport

Rock Island
Moline

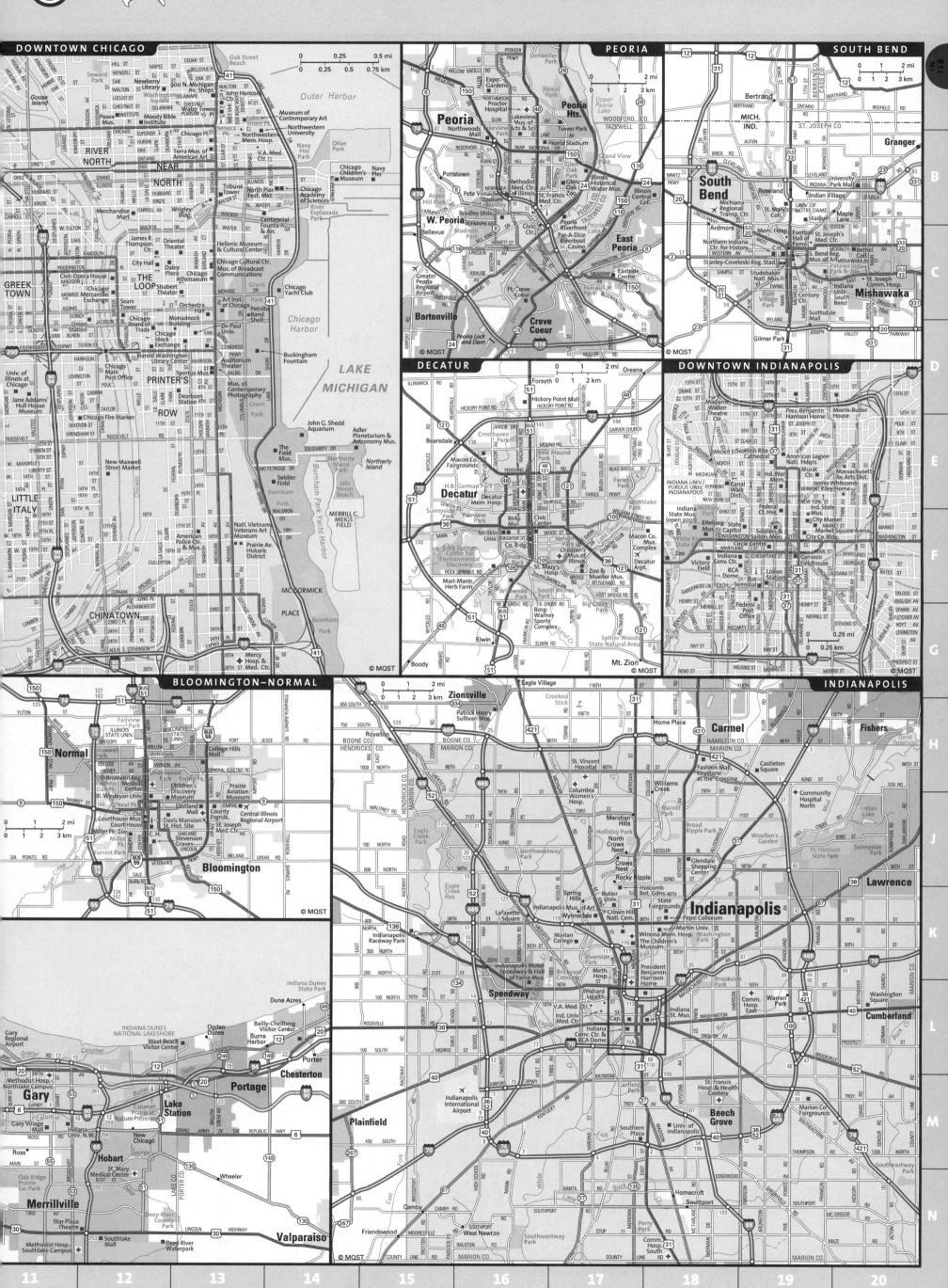

MI 10 20
KM 10 20

N

© MapQuest.com, Inc.

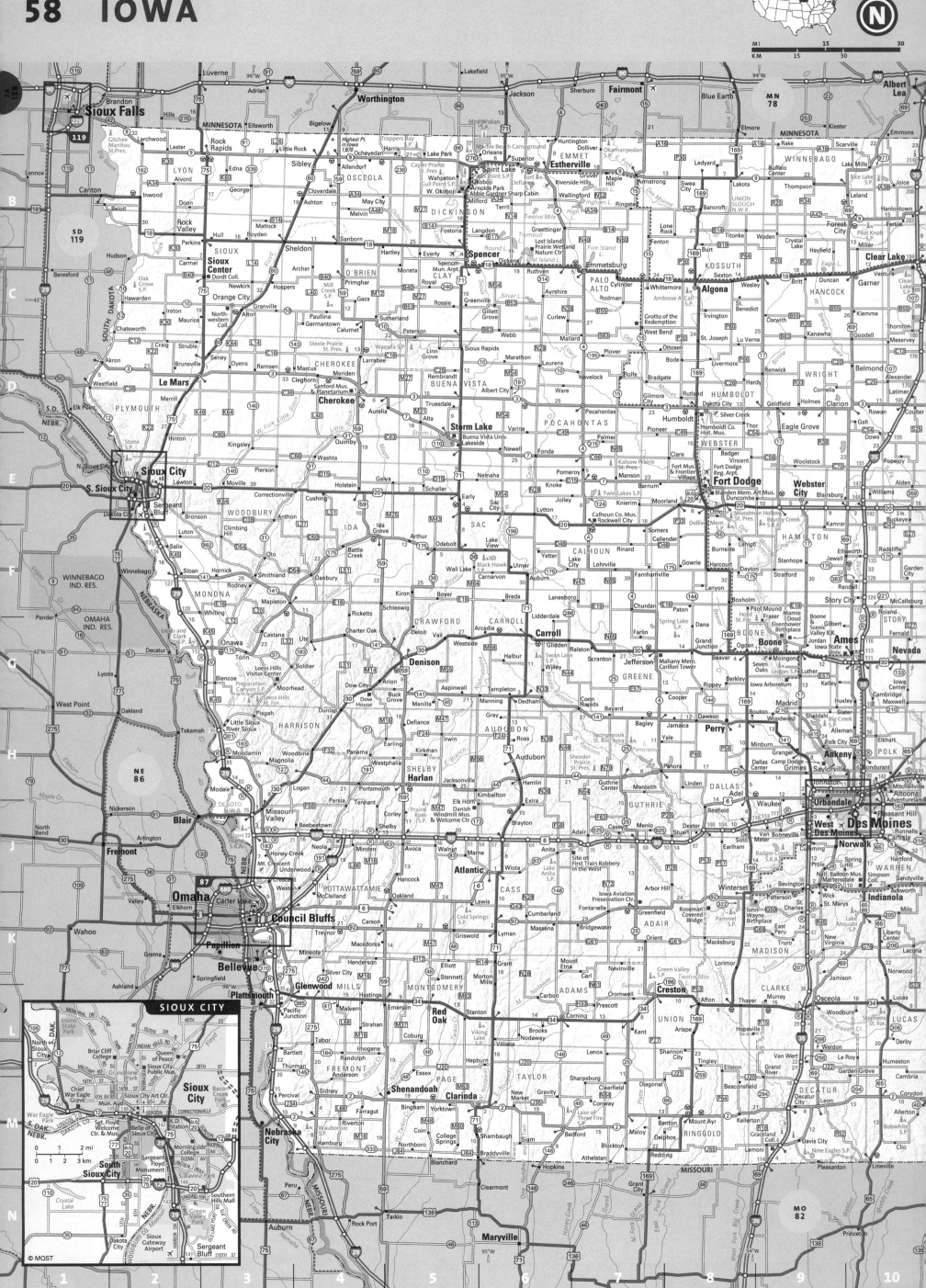

	AMES	BURLINGTON	CARROLL	CEDAR RAPIDS	COUNCIL BLUFFS	CRESTON	DAVENPORT	DECORAH	DES MOINES	DUBUQUE	FORT DODGE	IOWA CITY	MARSHALLTOWN	MASON CITY	OTTUMWA	SIOUX CITY	SPENCER	WATERLOO
COUNCIL BLUFFS	165	323	101	261		99	303	347	130	327	160	245	181	258	216	101	157	238
DES MOINES	34	157	90	129	130	81	171	215		196	94	113	49	126	86	202	188	106
IOWA CITY	136	82	195	28	245	195	59	131	113	84	196		98	157	83	316	267	78
SIOUX CITY	171	394	105	332	101	189	375	303	202	321	120	316	252	218	287		103	228
WATERLOO	95	157	160	53	238	189	137	79	106	93	108	78	58	79	125	228	189	

DRIVING DISTANCES IN MILES

SEE ALSO MILEAGE AND DRIVING TIME MAP ON PAGES 6-7

DES MOINES

CEDAR RAPIDS

© MapQuest.com, Inc.

MI 20 40
KM 20 40

N

NEBRASKA

COLORADO

OKLAHOMA

McCook

Major cities and towns: Goodland, Colby, Hays, Great Bend, Garden City, Dodge City, Ulysses, Liberal, Pratt

County names: CHEYENNE, RAWLINS, DECATUR, NORTON, PHILLIPS, SMITH, JEWELL, SHERMAN, THOMAS, SHERIDAN, GRAHAM, ROOKS, OSBORNE, MITCHELL, WALLACE, LOGAN, GOVE, TREGO, ELLIS, RUSSELL, LINCOLN, GREELEY, WICHITA, SCOTT, LANE, NESS, RUSH, BARTON, RICE, HAMILTON, KEARNY, FINNEY, HODGEMAN, PAWNEE, STAFFORD, QUIVIRA N.W.R., STANTON, GRANT, HASKELL, GRAY, FORD, EDWARDS, PRATT, MORTON, STEVENS, SEWARD, MEADE, CLARK, KIOWA, COMANCHE, BARBER

CENTRAL TIME ZONE / MOUNTAIN TIME ZONE

Mt. Sunflower Highest Pt. in Kansas 4,039'

Geographic Center of the 48 Contiguous States

Monument Rocks Natl. Landmark

KIRWIN N.W.R.

CIMARRON NATL. GRASSLAND

Mid America Air Mus.

Yellow Brick Road

MANHATTAN

Kansas State Univ. Stadium, Fred Bramlage Coliseum, Goodnow House, Kansas State Univ., Kansas Christian College, Manhattan Town Center, Sunset Zoo, Cico Park, Frank Anneberg Sports Complex, Warner Memorial Park

0 1 2 mi
0 1 2 3 km

© MQST

TOPEKA

Historic Ward-Meade Park, Menninger Foundation, Kansas Mus. of Hist., Topeka Zoo, Gage Park, State Capitol, Brown v. Board of Ed. N.H.S., Washburn Univ., Mulvane Art Mus., Kansas Expocentre, Forbes Field, Combat Air Mus.

0 1 2 mi
0 1 2 3 km

© MQST

LAWRENCE

Tanger Factory Outlet Ctr., Lawrence Memorial Hospital, Old West Lawrence Hist. Dist., City Hall, Watkins Comm. Museum, Spencer Mus. of Art, Museum of Anthropology, Lied Center, UNIVERSITY OF KANSAS, Allen Fieldhouse, Memorial Stadium, Haskell Indian Nations Univ., Naismith Valley, Douglas County Fairgrounds

0 0.5 1 mi
0 0.5 1.5 km

	ARKANSAS CITY	ATCHISON	COLBY	DODGE CITY	EMPORIA	GARDEN CITY	GREAT BEND	HAYS	HUTCHINSON	INDEPENDENCE	IOLA	KANSAS CITY	LAWRENCE	LIBERAL	MANHATTAN	SALINA	TOPEKA	WICHITA
DODGE CITY	141	107	315		238	52	83	106	120	270	265	333	298	83	232	164	271	153
KANSAS CITY	247	50	369	333	106	373	250	261	240	162	105		35	402	117	172	61	192
SALINA	151	160	200	164	118	204	81	93	68	206	187	172	137	247	72		111	92
TOPEKA	193	49	308	271	58	311	188	200	178	135	100	61	26	347	55	111		137
WICHITA	61	186	289	153	85	205	119	181	51	118	92	192	159	210	131	92	137	

DRIVING DISTANCES IN MILES

SEE ALSO MILEAGE AND DRIVING TIME MAP ON PAGES 6–7

DRIVING DISTANCES IN MILES

	ASHLAND	BOWLING GREEN	CINCINNATI OH	ELIZABETHTOWN	FRANKFORT	GLASGOW	HAZARD	HENDERSON	HOPKINSVILLE	LEXINGTON	LONDON	LOUISVILLE	MAYFIELD	MAYSVILLE	MIDDLESBORO	OWENSBORO	PADUCAH	PIKEVILLE
BOWLING GREEN	274		212	70	161	36	200	107	63	157	145	112	146	222	203	76	135	265
LEXINGTON	119	157	85	89	29	138	120	201	215		77	80	273	67	136	183	262	142
LOUISVILLE	194	112	100	44	54	92	194	123	170	80	156		228	114	214	109	217	217
OWENSBORO	300	76	206	95	161	111	275	30	48	221	109	138	248	279		127	323	
PADUCAH	379	135	317	175	266	173	337	121	72	262	283	217	24	327	373	127		402

SEE ALSO MILEAGE AND DRIVING TIME MAP ON PAGES 6–7

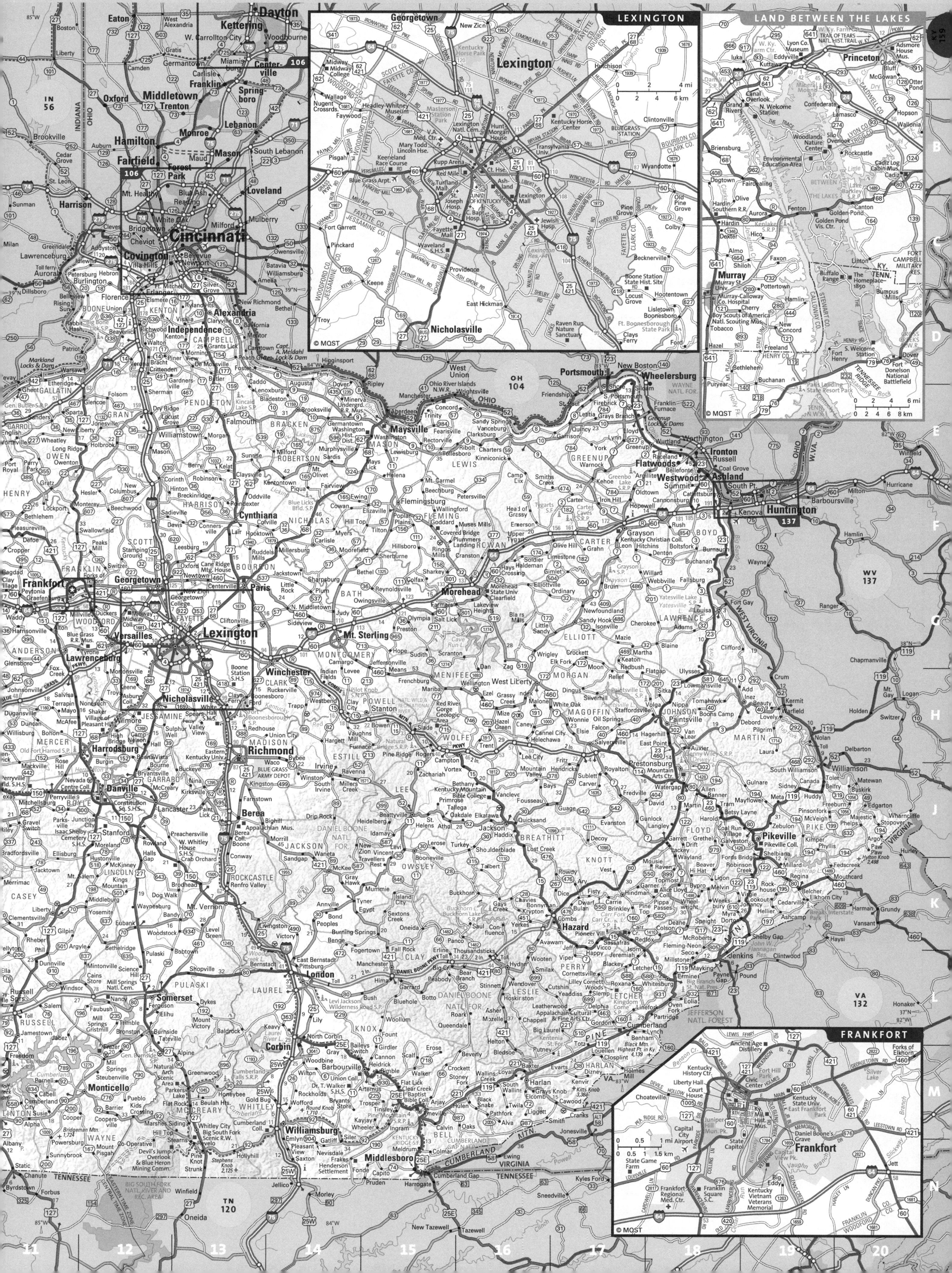

LEXINGTON

LAND BETWEEN THE LAKES

FRANKFORT

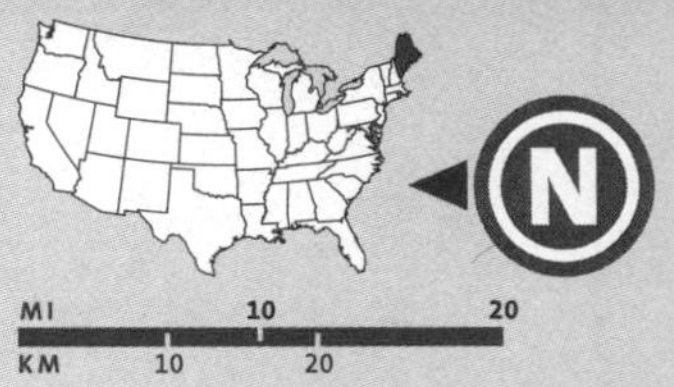
MI 10 20
KM 10 20
N

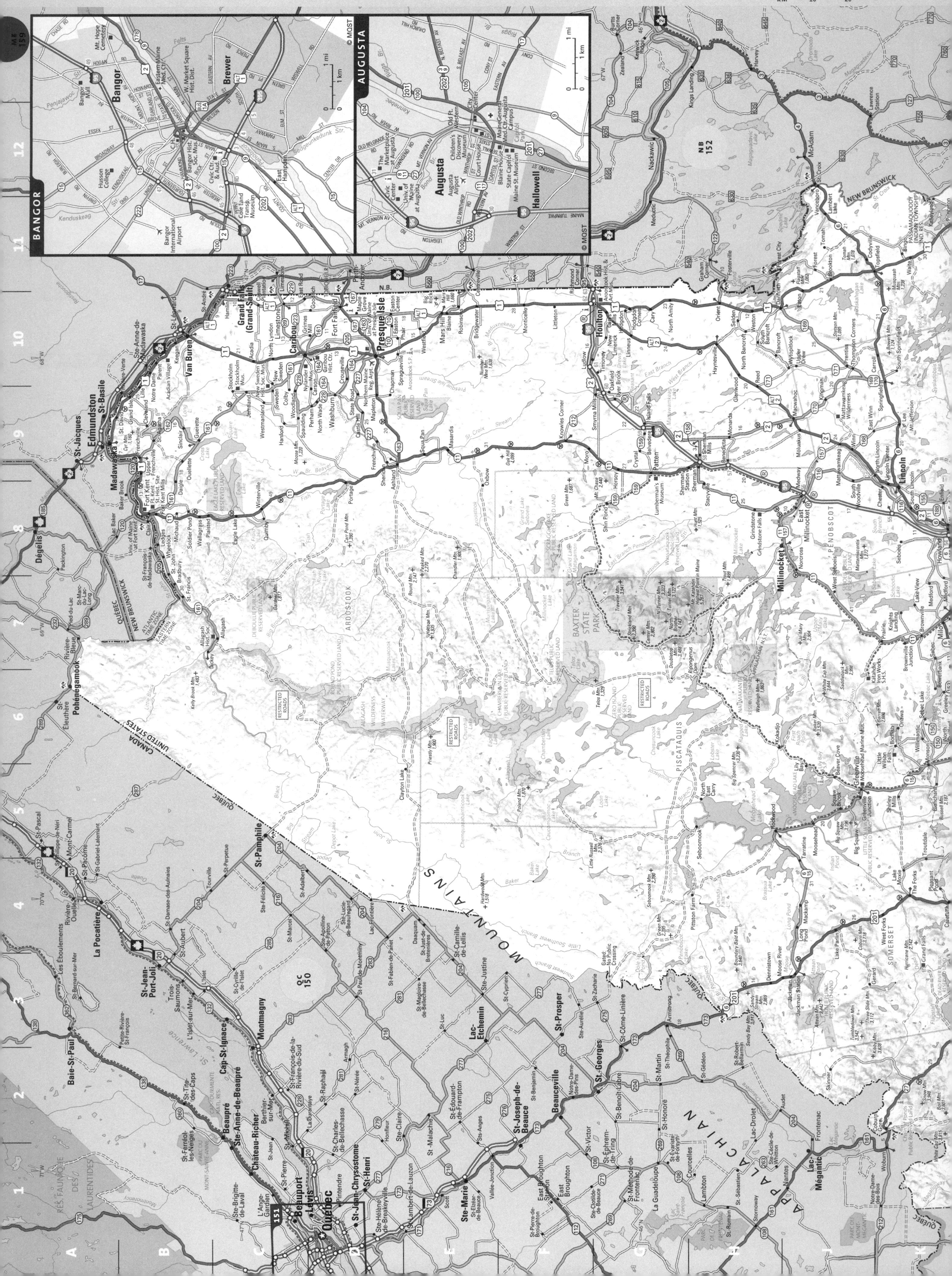
BANGOR
AUGUSTA
Bangor
Brewer
Augusta
Hallowell
Bangor International Airport
Edmundston
St-Jacques
St-Basile
Madawaska
Fort Kent
Van Buren
Grand Falls (Grand-Sault)
Caribou
Presque Isle
Washburn
Mars Hill
Houlton
Patten
Millinocket
East Millinocket
Lincoln
Greenville
Rockwood
Jackman
Lac-Mégantic
St-Georges
Beauceville
St-Joseph-de-Beauce
Lac-Etchemin
Montmagny
Cap-St-Ignace
St-Jean-Port-Joli
La Pocatière
Rivière-Bleue
Pohénégamook
Dégelis
Québec
Lévis
Beauport
St-Henri
Ste-Marie
Baie-St-Paul
BAXTER STATE PARK
ALLAGASH WILDERNESS WATERWAY
APPALACHIAN
MOUNTAINS
CANADA
UNITED STATES
QUÉBEC
NEW BRUNSWICK
AROOSTOOK
PISCATAQUIS
PENOBSCOT
SOMERSET
St. Lawrence
Moosehead Lake
Mt. Katahdin Highest Point in Maine 5,267
NB 152
QC 150

	AUGUSTA	BANGOR	BAR HARBOR	BRUNSWICK	CALAIS	FARMINGTON	FORT KENT	GREENVILLE	HOULTON	LEWISTON	MACHIAS	MILLINOCKET	PORTLAND	PORTSMOUTH NH	PRESQUE ISLE	ROCKLAND	SACO	WATERVILLE
AUGUSTA		77	120	32	173	65	269	99	196	35	161	149	58	110	236	43	74	20
BANGOR	77		45	106	97	80	195	74	122	108	85	75	131	184	162	58	147	56
CALAIS	173	97	112	203		177	189	160	91	205	85	112	228	281	133	155	244	153
HOULTON	196	122	166	226	91	200	98	155		228	126	73	251	304	42	182	267	176
PORTLAND	58	131	251	27	228	81	324	153	251	36	216	203		53	291	78	16	84

DRIVING DISTANCES IN MILES

SEE ALSO MILEAGE AND DRIVING TIME MAP ON PAGES 6–7

© MapQuest.com, Inc.

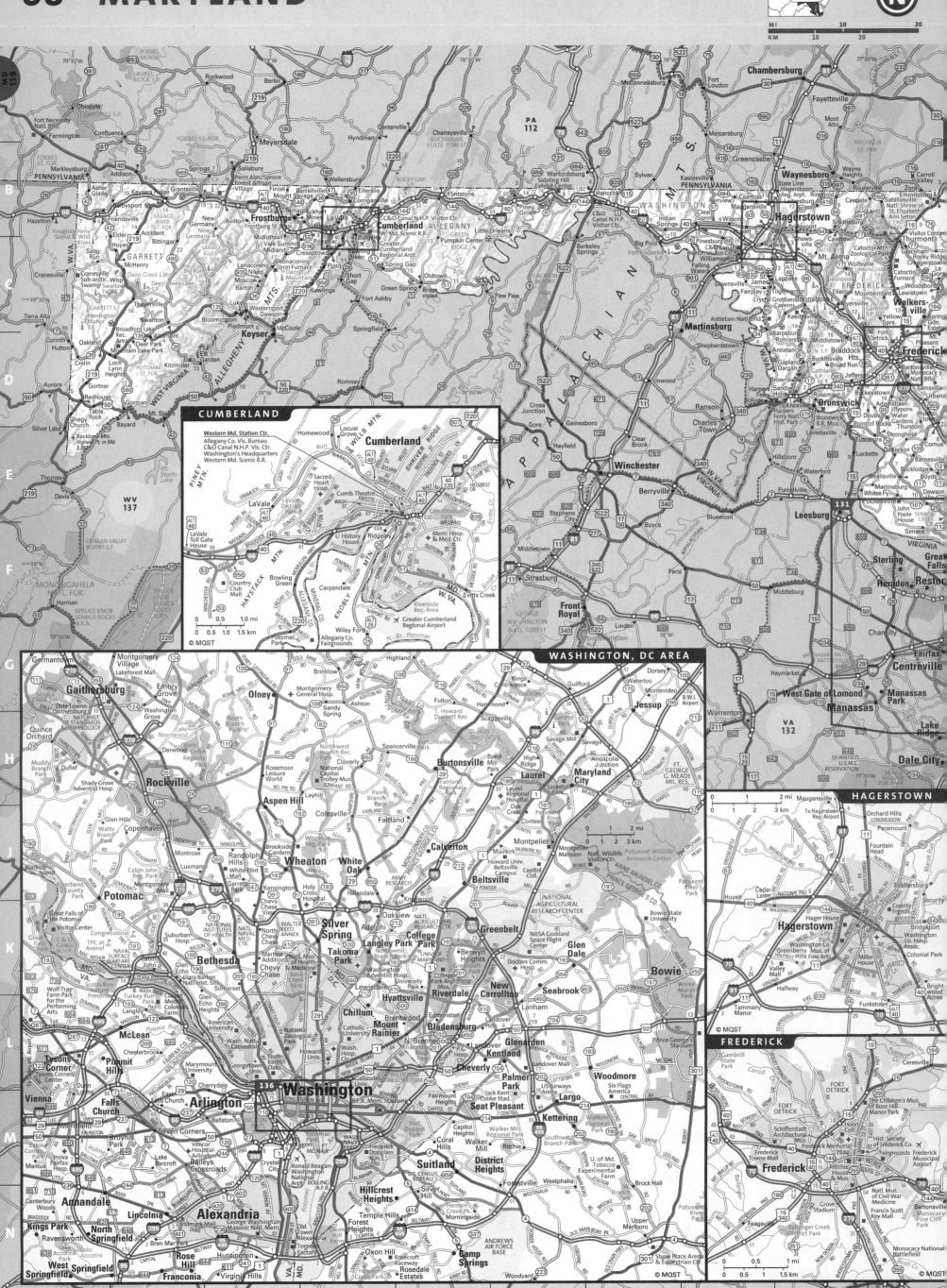

	ANNAPOLIS	ABERDEEN	BALTIMORE	CAMBRIDGE	CHESTERTOWN	CUMBERLAND	EASTON	FREDERICK	HAGERSTOWN	HANCOCK	LEXINGTON PARK	OCEAN CITY	POCOMOKE CITY	ROCKVILLE	ST. CHARLES	SALISBURY	WASHINGTON, DC	WESTMINSTER
ANNAPOLIS	54		25	55	45	162	38	73	98	124	66	108	112	47	47	83	31	56
BALTIMORE	35	25		78	68	140	61	51	76	102	95	131	135	45	57	106	38	39
HAGERSTOWN	109	98	76	153	143	67	136	28		29	142	206	211	54	103	182	70	50
SALISBURY	124	83	106	32	81	246	47	156	182	207	149	30	29	130	130		115	138
WASHINGTON, DC	71	31	38	87	76	134	70	44	70	96	63	139	144	19	25	115		53

DRIVING DISTANCES IN MILES

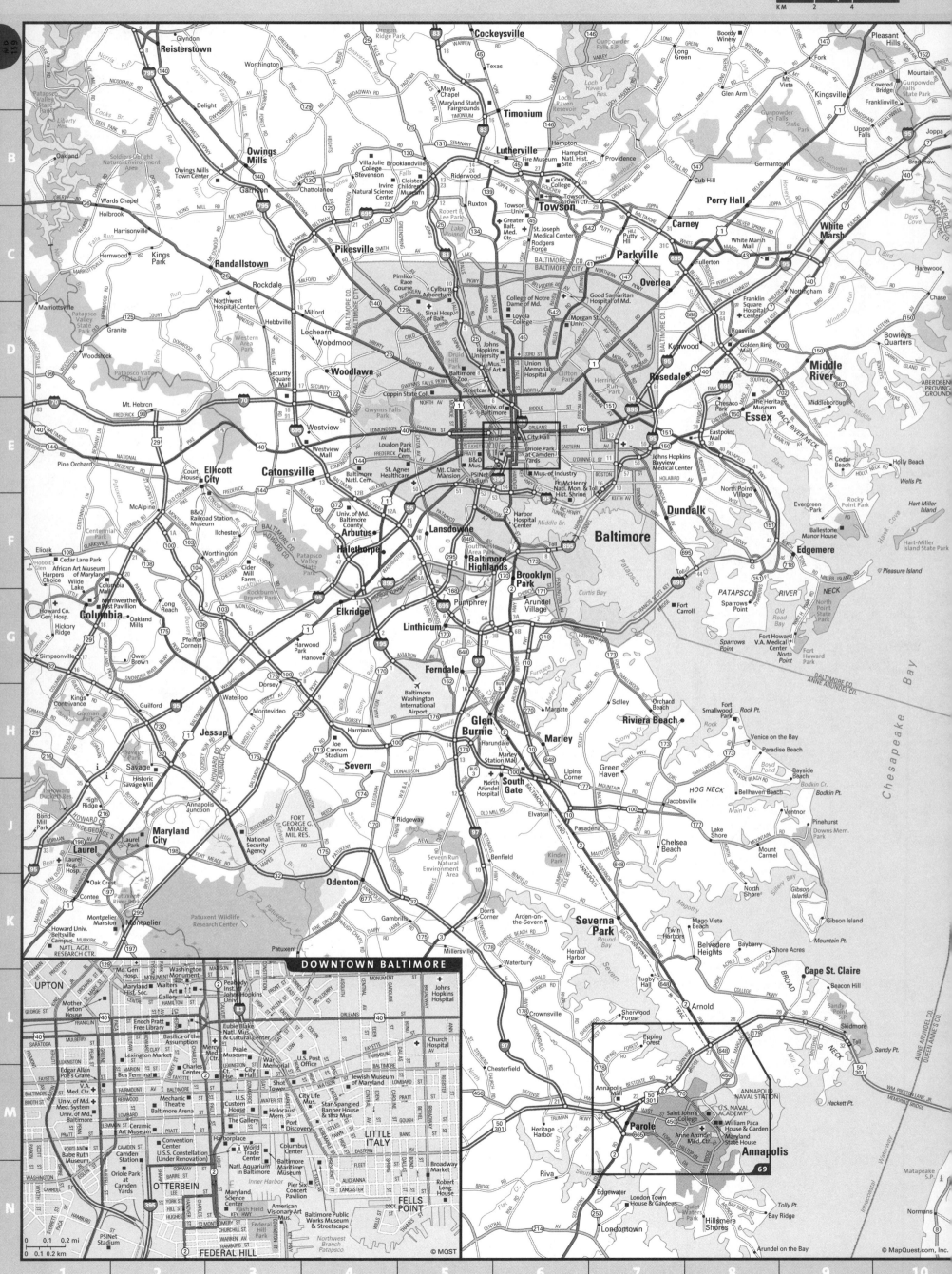

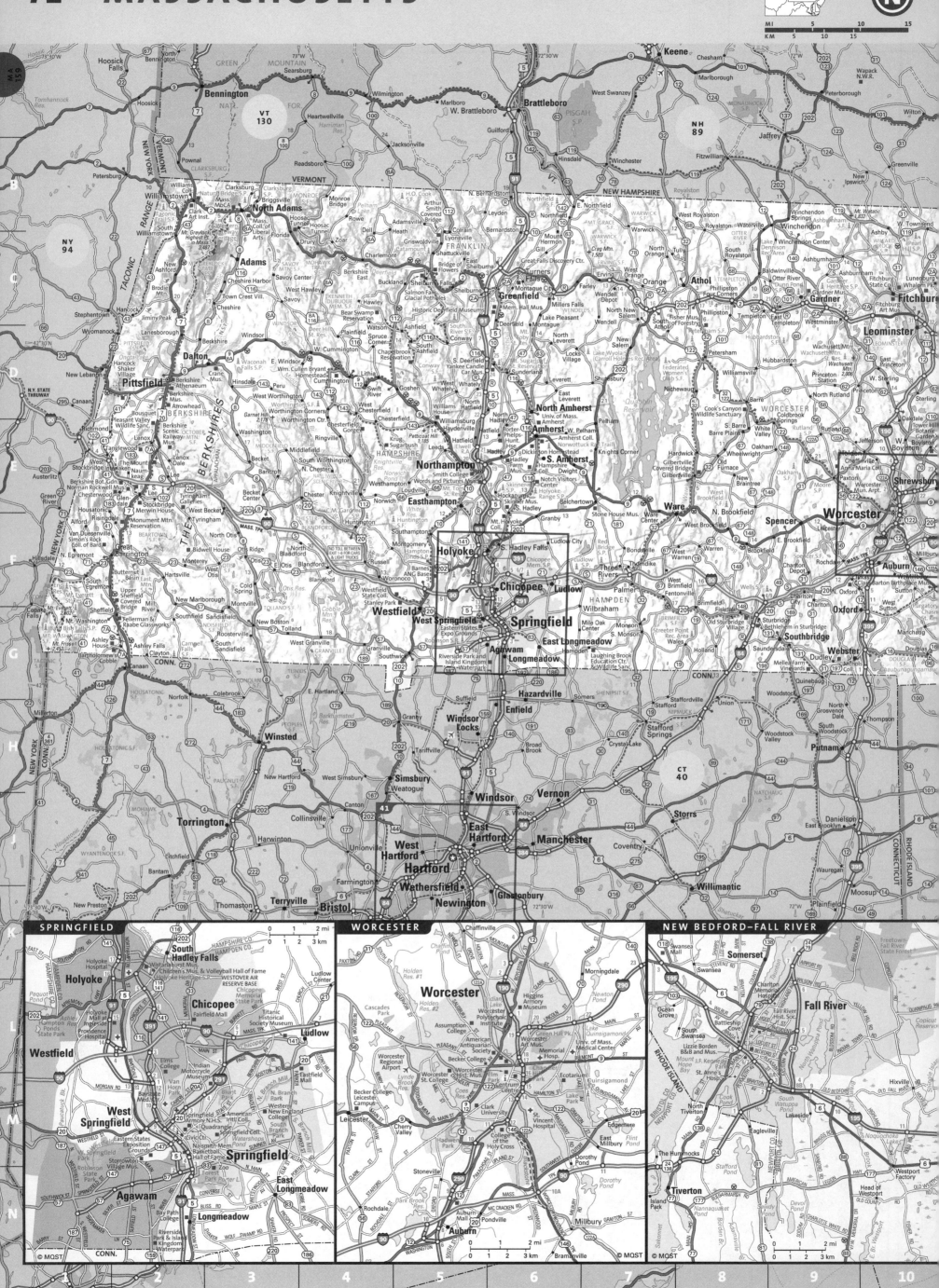

	BOSTON BROCKTON	FALL RIVER	FALMOUTH	FITCHBURG	GLOUCESTER	GREENFIELD	HYANNIS	LOWELL	NEW BEDFORD	NORTH ADAMS	NORTHAMPTON	PITTSFIELD	PLYMOUTH	PROVIDENCE RI	SPRINGFIELD	WORCESTER
BOSTON	26	53	72	49	35	93	72	31	60	133	105	140	41	52	117	95	46
NEW BEDFORD	60	38	16	41	101	95	136	45	86		189	137	172	43	33	91	127	78
PITTSFIELD	140	153	153	189	101	174	52	193	142	172	17	41		166	138	239	55	101
SPRINGFIELD	95	108	92	143	85	129	40	148	96	127	72	18	55	120	75		193	55
WORCESTER	46	59	58	95	31	80	58	99	44	78	97	65	101	72	43	144	55	

DRIVING DISTANCES IN MILES   SEE ALSO MILEAGE AND DRIVING TIME MAP ON PAGES 6–7

LOWELL

© MapQuest.com, Inc.

NORTHWESTERN MICHIGAN

LAKE SUPERIOR

LAKE HURON

LAKE MICHIGAN

ISLE ROYALE NATIONAL PARK

SAGINAW

© MapQuest.com, Inc.

	Alpena	Ann Arbor	Benton Harbor	Cadillac	Detroit	Escanaba	Flint	Grand Rapids	Houghton	Kalamazoo	Lansing	Mackinaw City	Marquette	Muskegon	Port Huron	Saginaw	Sault Ste Marie	Traverse City
DETROIT	242	42	186	209		438	62	153	556	136	82	291	455	191	58	97	346	257
GRAND RAPIDS	261	129	78	89	153	391	112		510	53	67	244	408	40	176	144	299	141
LANSING	230	63	126	131	86	375	53	67	493	76		228	391	105	117	86	282	173
MACKINAW CITY	94	281	323	145	291	149	230	244	268	402	228		166	248	293	198	57	106
MARQUETTE	257	444	487	309	455	65	393	408	102	466	391	166		412	457	361	163	269

DRIVING DISTANCES IN MILES   SEE ALSO MILEAGE AND DRIVING TIME MAP ON PAGES 6-7

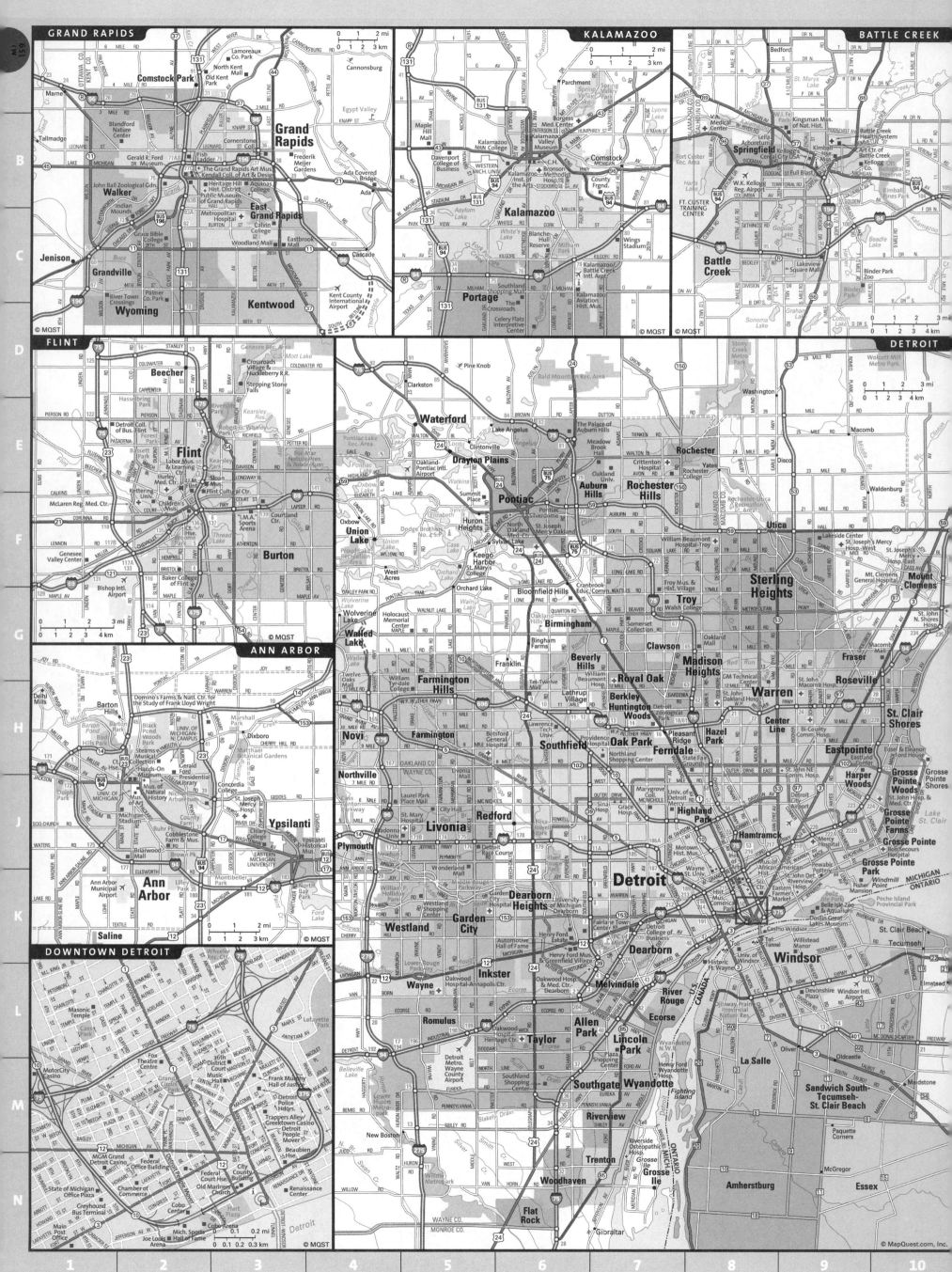

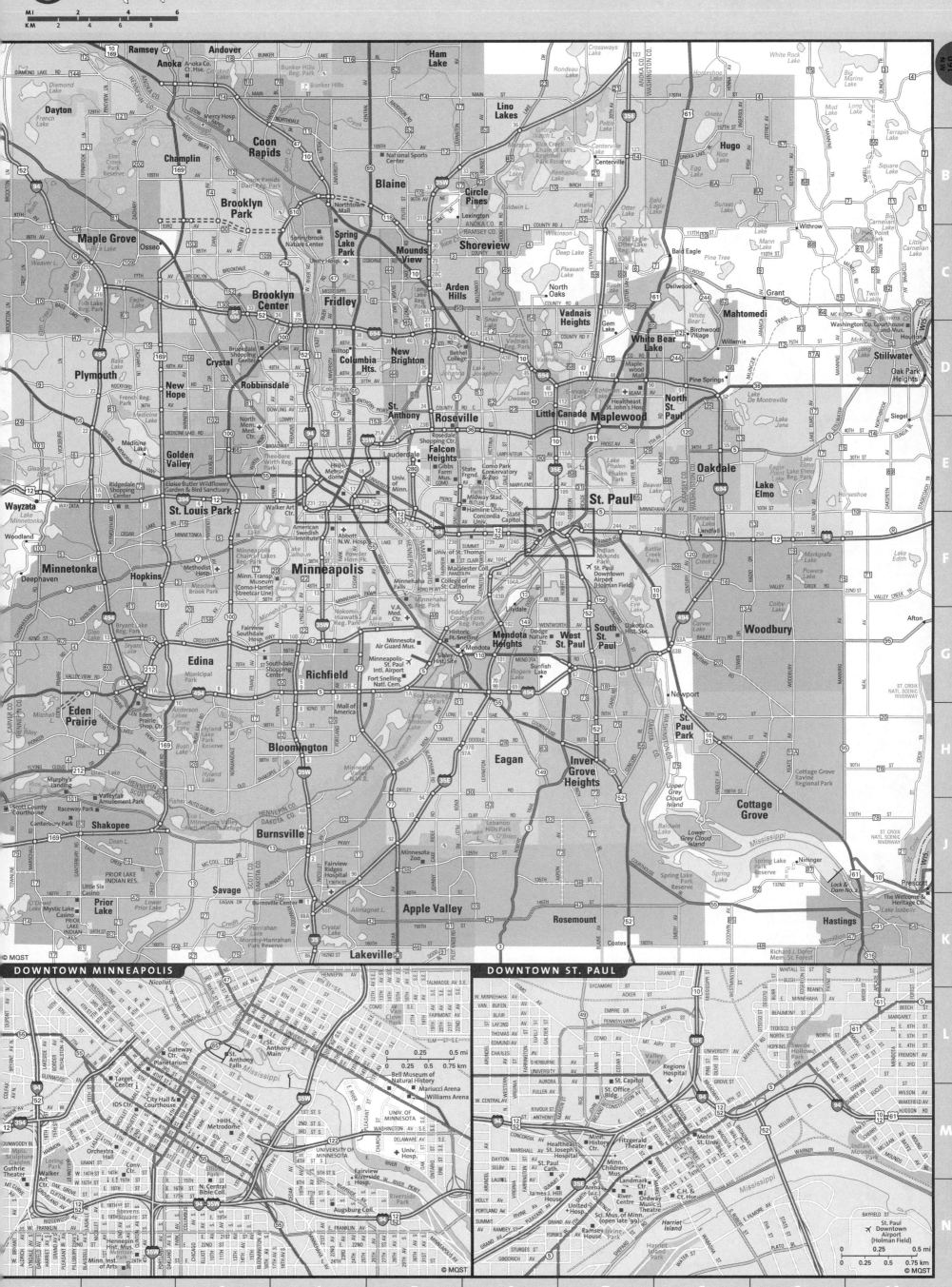

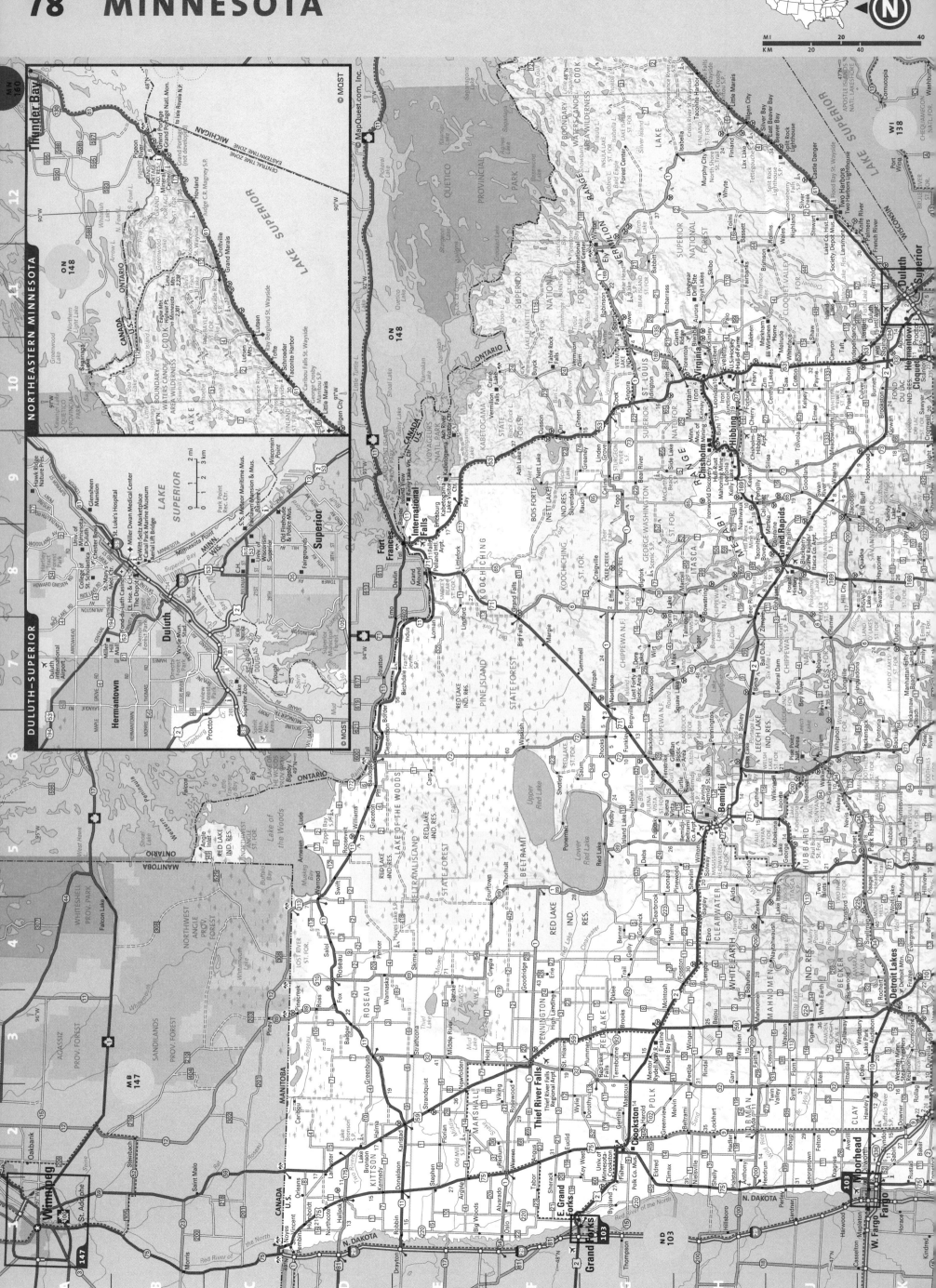

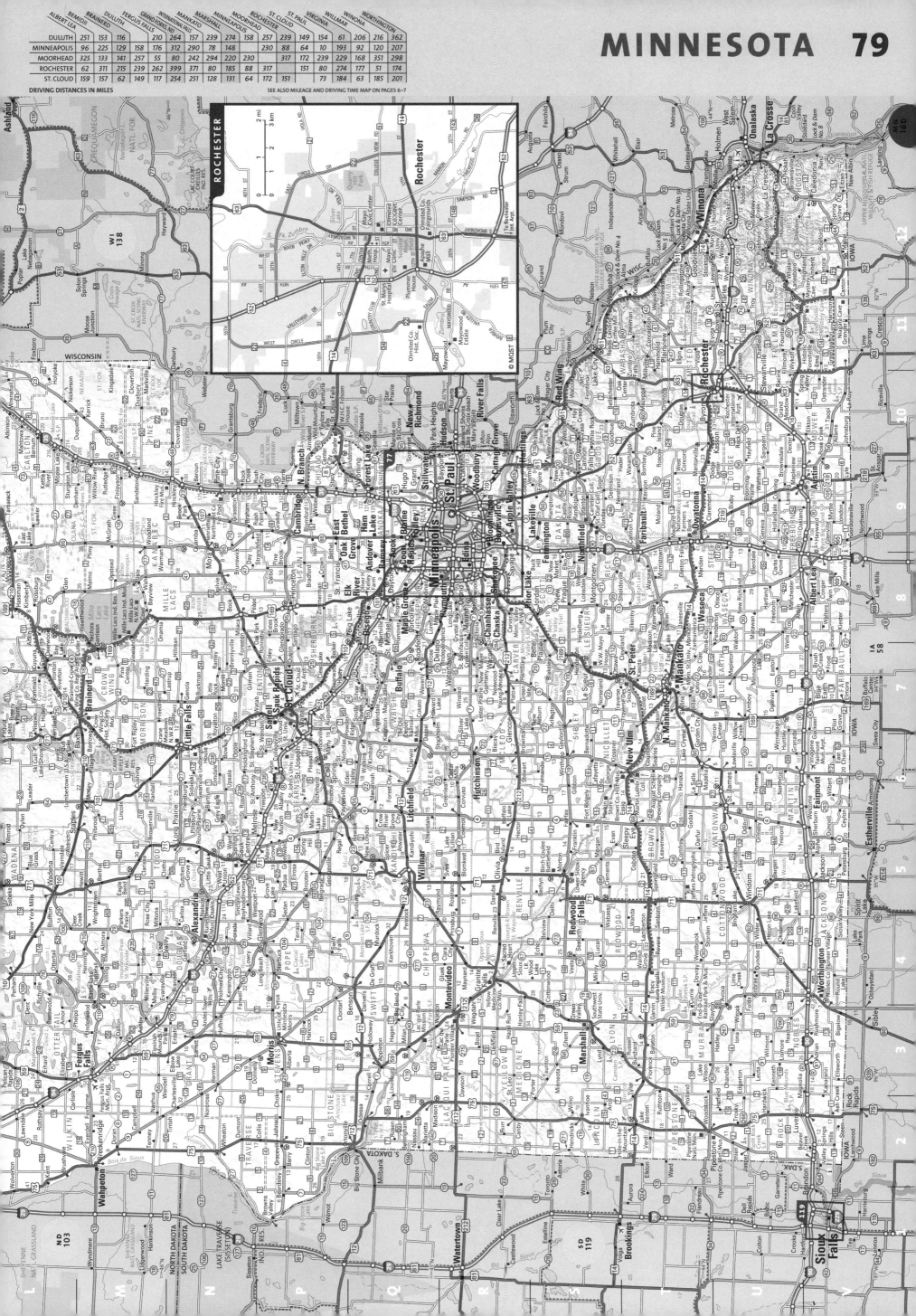

	ALBERT LEA	BEMIDJI	BRAINERD	DULUTH	FERGUS FALLS	GRAND FORKS, ND	INTERNATIONAL FALLS	MANKATO	MARSHALL	MINNEAPOLIS	MOORHEAD	ROCHESTER	ST. CLOUD	ST. PAUL	VIRGINIA	WILLMAR	WINONA	WORTHINGTON
DULUTH	251	153	116		210	264	157	274	158	154	239	274	157	158	61	206	216	362
MINNEAPOLIS	96	225	129	158	176	312	290	78	148		230	88	64	10	193	92	120	207
MOORHEAD	325	133	141	257	55	80	242	294	220	230		317	172	239	229	168	351	298
ROCHESTER	62	311	215	239	262	399	371	80	185	88	317		151	80	274	171	51	174
ST. CLOUD	159	157	62	149	117	254	251	131	64	172	151	73		184	63	185	201	

DRIVING DISTANCES IN MILES

SEE ALSO MILEAGE AND DRIVING TIME MAP ON PAGES 6–7

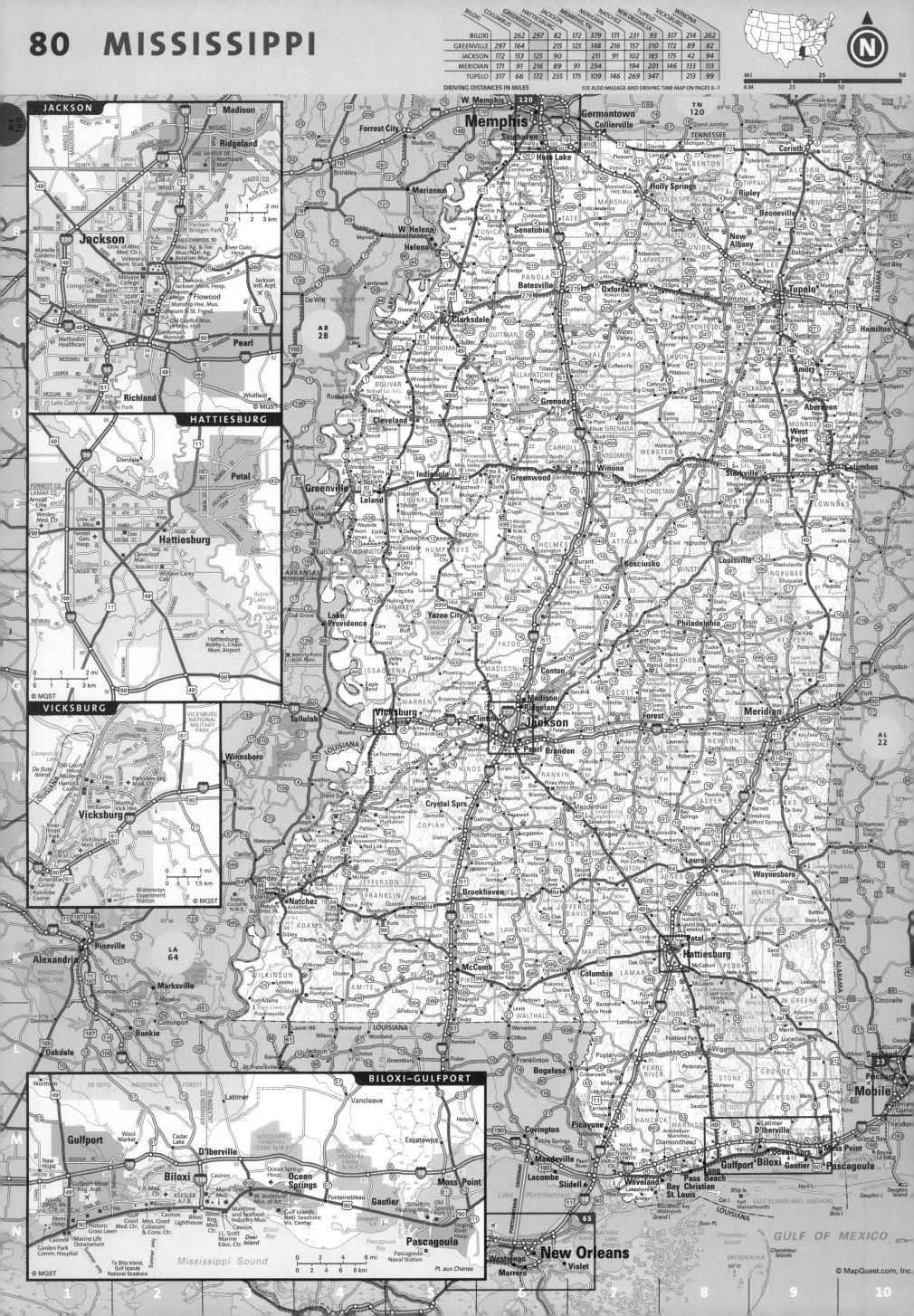

80 MISSISSIPPI

	BILOXI	COLUMBUS	GREENVILLE	HATTIESBURG	JACKSON	MEMPHIS, TN	MERIDIAN	NATCHEZ	NEW ORLEANS, LA	TUPELO	VICKSBURG	WINONA
BILOXI		262	297	82	172	379	171	231	93	317	214	262
GREENVILLE	297	164		215	125	148	216	157	310	172	89	82
JACKSON	172	153	125	90		211	91	102	185	175	42	94
MERIDIAN	171	91	216	89	91	234		194	201	146	133	113
TUPELO	317	66	172	235	175	109	146	269	347		213	99

DRIVING DISTANCES IN MILES   SEE ALSO MILEAGE AND DRIVING TIME MAP ON PAGES 6–7

© MapQuest.com, Inc.

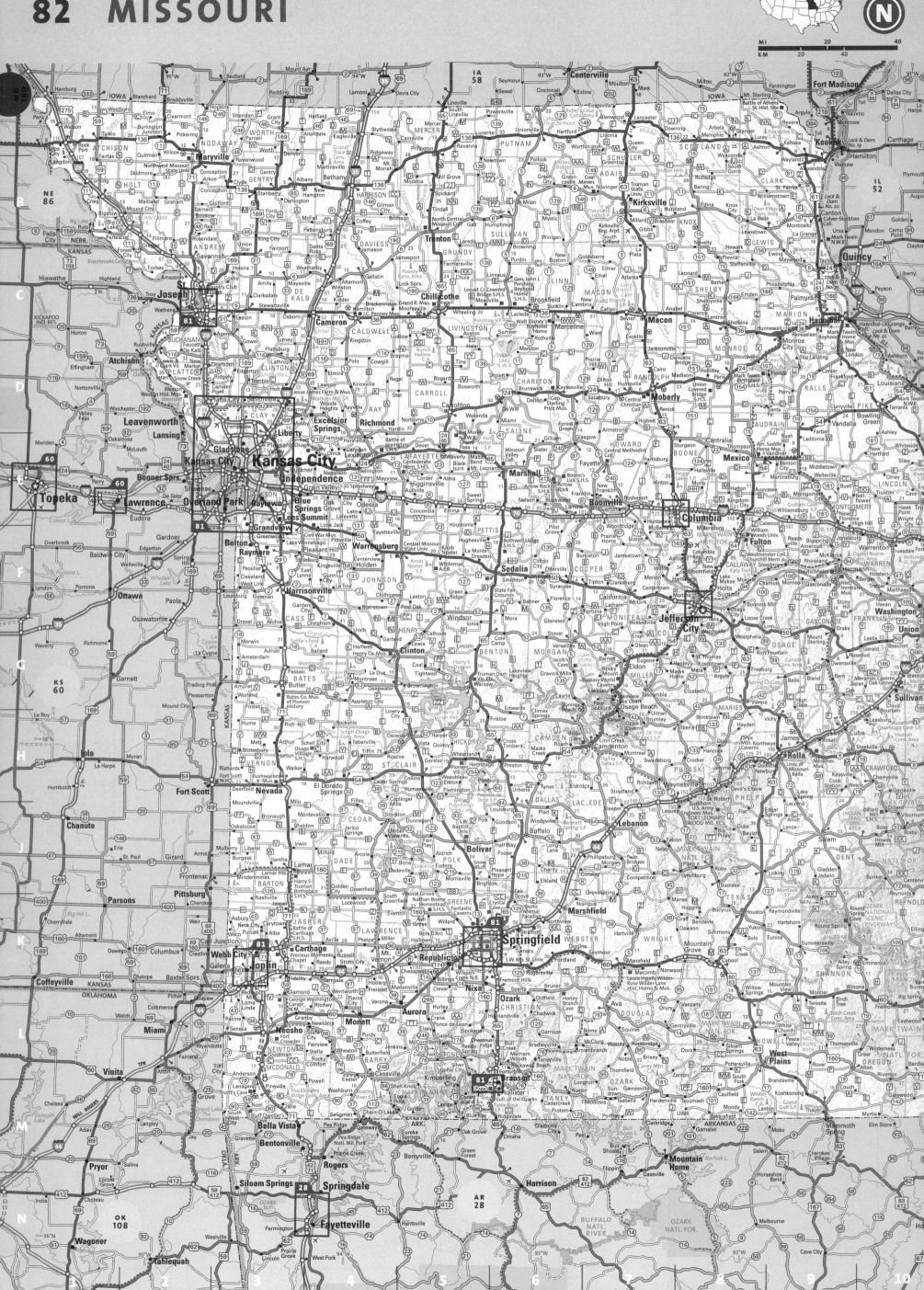

	BRANSON	CAPE GIRARDEAU	CHILLICOTHE	COLUMBIA	HANNIBAL	JEFFERSON CITY	JOPLIN	KANSAS CITY	KIRKSVILLE	NEVADA	POPLAR BLUFF	ROLLA	ST. JOSEPH	ST. LOUIS	SEDALIA	SIKESTON	SPRINGFIELD	WEST PLAINS
CAPE GIRARDEAU	347		357	234	228	243	382	363	322	374	75	205	419	120	303	36	307	175
COLUMBIA	203	234	124		101	32	238	129	89	206	269	97	185	123	69	265	131	194
KANSAS CITY	210	363	92	129	230	161	165		161	104	398	226	56	252	97	394	169	278
ST. LOUIS	249	120	247	123	117	132	284	252	212	276	156	107	308		111	209	204	
SPRINGFIELD	41	307	200	163	241	131	70	169	251	95	191	110	225	209	108	238		109

DRIVING DISTANCES IN MILES

SEE ALSO MILEAGE AND DRIVING TIME MAP ON PAGES 6–7

MI · 25 · 50
KM · 25 · 50

© MapQuest.com, Inc.

	BOZEMAN	BROWNING	BUTTE	DILLON	GLASGOW	GLENDIVE	GREAT FALLS	HAVRE	HELENA	KALISPELL	LEWISTOWN	MILES CITY	MISSOULA	SHELBY	SHERIDAN, WY	WEST GLACIER	WEST YELLOWSTONE
BILLINGS	141	346	223	253	277	217	222	235	454	125	144	340	304	131	474	232
BUTTE	223	81		241		63	430	439	153	271	71	232	247	367	118	235	354	252	162
GREAT FALLS	222	176	124	153	215	277	351		118	85	222	109	329	199	82	353	192	257
HELENA	235	94	174	71	132	362	452	85	203		195	192	379	114	168	366	216	174
MISSOULA	340	199	201	118	171	476	557	199	317	114	116	306	484		227	471	136	279

DRIVING DISTANCES IN MILES   SEE ALSO MILEAGE AND DRIVING TIME MAP ON PAGES 6-7

N

MI 20 40
KM 20 40

Rapid City 119

Newcastle
Hill City
Mt. Rushmore Natl. Mem.
BLACK HILLS NATL. FOR.
Custer
CUSTER S.P.
Jewell Cave Natl. Mon.
WIND CAVE NATL. PARK
Hot Springs
119

Wall
BUFFALO GAP NATL. GRASSLAND
Kadoka
Murdo
Vivian
Presho
Kennebec
FORT PIERRE NATL. GRASSLAND
LOWER BRULE INDIAN RES.

BADLANDS NATL. PARK
Wanblee
White River
SD 119

Kyle

PINE RIDGE INDIAN RESERVATION
Porcupine
Parmelee
Mission
Winner
Colome

Oelrichs
Wounded Knee
Martin
Rosebud
ROSEBUD INDIAN RES.
St. Francis
Olsonville

Pine Ridge
SOUTH DAKOTA
Tuthill
Lacreek N.W.R.

WY 140
Van Tassel
Warbonnet Monument
OGLALA NATL. GRASSLAND
Whiteclay
Merriman
Eli
Cody
Kilgore
Crookston
Sandhills Mus.
Cherry Co. Hist. Mus.
Sparks
Norden
Springview

Toadstool Geologic Park
Harrison
Fort Robinson
Chadron
Chadron Mun. Arpt.
Museum of the Fur Trade
Chadron S.P.
Chadron State Coll.
Gordon
Cowboy Museum
Nenzel
COTTONWOOD LAKE ST. REC. AREA
Valentine
FORT NIOBRARA N.W.R.
Smith Falls S.P.

Crawford
Nebraska Natl. For.
Pine Ridge N.R.A.
Whitney
Hay Springs
Clinton
Rushville
SAMUEL R. McKELVIE NATL. FOR.
Niobrara Valley Preserve
Keller Park St. Rec. Area
Wood Lake
Ainsworth

SIOUX
Marsland
Box Butte St. Rec. Area
Box Butte Res.
Walgren Lake St. Rec. Area
SHERIDAN
CHERRY
VALENTINE N.W.R.
Johnstown
Long Pine
Long Pine St. Rec. Area

Agate Fossil Beds Natl. Mon.
Hemingford
Mari Sandoz St. Hist. Marker
Big Hill 4,144
BROWN
Brownlee
Elsmere

BOX BUTTE
Berea
SURVEY VALLEY
SAND HILLS
Giant Hill 3,400

Torrington
Carhenge
Alliance
Knight Mus. of High Plains Heritage
Alliance Mun. Arpt.
Antioch
Lakeside
Ellsworth
Bingham
Ashby
Whitman
Mullen
Seneca
Purdum
Halsey
Brewster

Henry
Morrill
Mitchell
North Platte N.W.R.
Angora
Hyannis
Wild Horse Hill 4,204
GRANT
HOOKER
THOMAS
Thedford
Scott Lookout Tower
NEBRASKA NATL. FOR.
BLAINE
Dunning

Huntley
Lyman
Riverside Zoo
Scottsbluff
Scotts Bluff Natl. Mon.
Gering
Melbeta
Bayard
MORRILL
CRESCENT LAKE N.W.R.
Arthur
ARTHUR
Tryon
McPHERSON
LOGAN
Stapleton
Gandy
Arnold
Merna
CUSTER
Anselmo

Hawk Springs Res.
William B. Heilig Field
Lake Minatare St. Rec. Area
Minatare
North Platte Valley Mus.
McGrew
Angora
MOUNTAIN TIME ZONE
CENTRAL TIME ZONE
Ringgold

Lagrange
SCOTTS BLUFF
Wildcat Hills S.R.A.
Chimney Rock N.H.S.
Bridgeport
Bridgeport St. Rec. Area
Northport
Pioneer Trails Mus.
Broadwater
GARDEN
Courthouse Mus. & Haybale Church
Flats
Arnold St. Rec. Area
Callaway

Harrisburg
BANNER
Redington
Courthouse Rock and Jail Rock
Lisco
Oshkosh
Bluewater Battlefield
Milburn
Victoria Springs S.R.A.
Middle Loup

Pine Bluffs
Bushnell
Kimball
Dix
CHEYENNE
Dalton
Gurley
LAKE McCONAUGHY ST. REC. AREA
Lewellen
Ash Hollow St. Hist. Park
KEITH
Lake McConaughy
Kingsley Dam
Keystone
Lake Ogallala
Sarben
Sutherland
Hershey
North Platte
North Platte Reg. Arpt.
Maxwell
Brady
Pony Express Sta.
Oconto

Kimball
Oliver S.R.A.
Potter
Brownson
Fort Sidney Mus. and Post Commander's Home Mus.
Sidney
Sunol
Lodgepole
Chappell
DEUEL
Brule
Ogallala
Front Street
Roscoe
Paxton
SUTHERLAND RES.
Sutherland St. Rec. Area
LINCOLN
Lake Maloney
Fort McPherson Natl. Cem.
Gothenburg
Robert Henri Mus.
Willow Island
Cozad
DAWSON
S.R.A.

Highest Point in Nebraska 5,424
KIMBALL
Colton
Lorenzo
Big Springs
PEETZ TABLE
Peetz
Julesburg
Sedgwick
Ovid
COLORADO
PERKINS
Grant
Madrid
Elsie
Wallace
Dickens
Wellfleet
Moorefield
Farnam
Gallagher Canyon S.R.A.
Johnson Lake S.R.A.

PAWNEE NATIONAL GRASSLAND
Proctor
Crook
Iliff
Fleming
Amherst
Brandon
Venango
Lamar
Grainton
HAYES
Maywood
Curtis
FRONTIER
Eustis
Elwood
Smithfield
GOSPER

Sterling
Stoneham
Atwood
Holyoke
CHASE
Imperial
Champion Lake S.R.A.
Champion
Enders
Enders Res.
Wauneta
Hayes Center
Stockville
Hugh Butler Lake
Harry Strunk Lake
Medicine Creek S.R.A.

Jackson Res.
Log Lane Village
CO 38
Akron
Yuma
Wray
Laird
Palisade
Hamlet
DUNDY
HITCHCOCK
Trenton
Culbertson
Indianola
RED WILLOW
Bartley
Cambridge
Edison
FURNAS

Fort Morgan
Brush
Champion Mill S.H.P.
Stratton
Massacre Canyon Mon.
Swanson Res.
Swanson S.R.A.
Red Willow St. Rec. Area
Sen. George Norris S.H.S.
McCook Mun. Arpt.
McCook
Museum of the High Plains
Indianola
Holbrook
Arapahoe
Hendley
Wilsonville
Beaver City Precept

Rock Creek Lake St. Rec. Area
Max
Parks
Benkelman
Haigler
Cedar Bluffs
Marion
Danbury
Lebanon
Beaver City

KANSAS
St. Francis
Wheeler
Oberlin
Norton
KS 60

© MapQuest.com, Inc.

WYOMING
SOUTH DAKOTA
COLORADO
KANSAS
MISSOURI

DAWES
PINE RIDGE

DRIVING DISTANCES IN MILES

	ALLIANCE	BEATRICE	CHADRON	COLUMBUS	GRAND ISLAND	HASTINGS	KEARNEY	LINCOLN	MC COOK	NEBRASKA CITY	NORFOLK	NORTH PLATTE	OGALLALA	OMAHA	O'NEILL	SCOTTSBLUFF	SOUTH SIOUX CITY	VALENTINE
GRAND ISLAND	317	135	373	64		23		95	147	144	105	143	196	150	111	318	179	210
LINCOLN	397	40	453	77	95	102	129		226	49	119	223	275	58	207	397	154	302
NORTH PLATTE	174	262	230	207	143	150	98	223	67	271	248		53	278	203	175	374	131
OMAHA	452	97	508	84	150	157	184	58	281	50	115	278	330		188	452	99	298
SCOTTSBLUFF	55	437	96	382	318	325	273	397	242	446	423	175	122	452	324		549	214

SEE ALSO MILEAGE AND DRIVING TIME MAP ON PAGES 6–7

Inset maps: **GRAND ISLAND** · **LINCOLN** · **OMAHA–COUNCIL BLUFFS**

	BEATTY	CARSON CITY	ELKO	ELY	FALLON	HAWTHORNE	LAS VEGAS	LAUGHLIN	RENO	TONOPAH	WEST WENDOVER	WINNEMUCCA
CARSON CITY	316		320	319	62	128	429	522	30	232	431	194
ELKO	349	320		180	255	300	424	517	291	257	111	127
ELY	259	319	180		257	299	244	338	317	167	120	273
LAS VEGAS	113	429	424	244	381	309		94	442	205	364	465
RENO	329	30	291	317	61	133	442	536		237	402	166

DRIVING DISTANCES IN MILES

SEE ALSO MILEAGE AND DRIVING TIME MAP ON PAGES 6-7

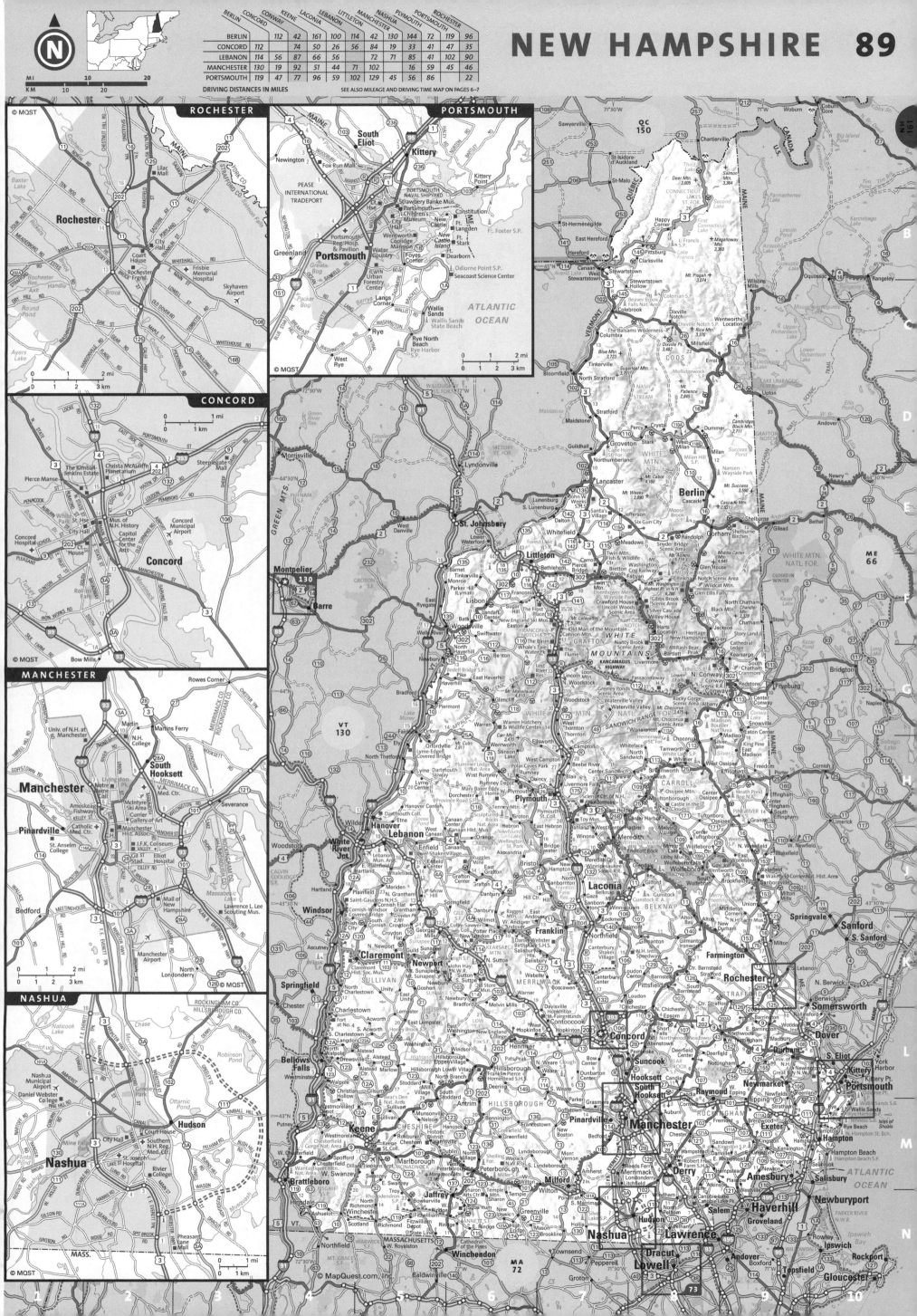

	BERLIN	CONCORD	CONWAY	KEENE	LACONIA	LEBANON	LITTLETON	MANCHESTER	NASHUA	PLYMOUTH	PORTSMOUTH	ROCHESTER
BERLIN		112	42	161	100	114	42	130	144	72	119	96
CONCORD	112		74	50	26	56	84	19	33	41	47	35
LEBANON	114	56	87	66	56		72	71	85	41	102	90
MANCHESTER	130	19	92	51	44	71	102		16	59	45	46
PORTSMOUTH	119	47	77	96	59	102	129	45	56	86		22

DRIVING DISTANCES IN MILES

SEE ALSO MILEAGE AND DRIVING TIME MAP ON PAGES 6–7

	CAMDEN	CAPE MAY	HACKENSACK	JERSEY CITY	LONG BRANCH	MORRISTOWN	NEW BRUNSWICK	NEW YORK, NY	NEWARK	NEWTON	PATERSON	PHILLIPSBURG	TOMS RIVER	TRENTON	VINELAND	WILMINGTON, DE
ATLANTIC CITY	61	41	133	120	82	126	94	125	114	159	128	62	120	54	77	47	86
NEW YORK, NY	125	92	155	12	5	55	32	34		11	54	16	91	67	75	55	119	120
NEWARK	114	82	144	15	5	45	18	23	11		51	18	80	57	65	45	109	109
PHILADELPHIA, PA	62	2	92	98	86	77	82	55	91	80	94	94		58	58	34	36	30
TRENTON	77	35	107	63	50	53	47	22	55	45	58	34	50		48	68	68

DRIVING DISTANCES IN MILES   SEE ALSO MILEAGE AND DRIVING TIME MAP ON PAGES 6–7

© MapQuest.com, Inc.

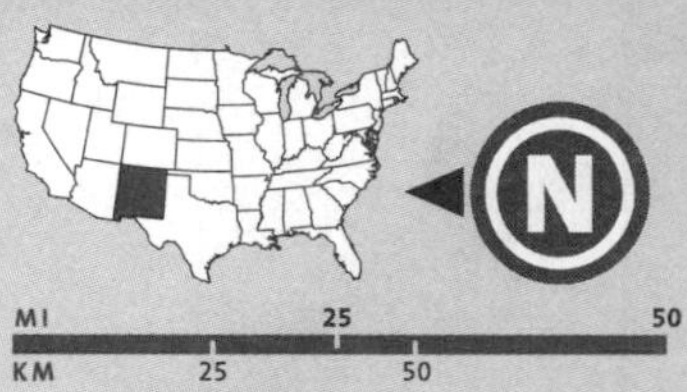
N
MI 25 50
KM 25 50

COLORADO
OKLAHOMA
TEXAS
ARIZONA
UTAH
CENTRAL TIME ZONE
MOUNTAIN TIME ZONE
Raton
Trinidad
Durango
Cortez
Farmington
Aztec
Bloomfield
Kirtland
Shiprock
Gallup
Window Rock
Chinle
Ft. Defiance
Taos
Española
Los Alamos
Santa Fe
Las Vegas
Tucumcari
Clovis
Portales
Santa Rosa
Roswell
Bernalillo
Rio Rancho
Albuquerque
Los Lunas
Belen
Socorro
Grants
Zuni Pueblo
Ruidoso
Truth or Consequences
WHITE SANDS MISSILE RANGE

	ALAMOGORDO	ALBUQUERQUE	CARLSBAD	CLOVIS	EL PASO, TX	FARMINGTON	GALLUP	HOBBS	LAS CRUCES	LAS VEGAS	LOS ALAMOS	RATON	ROSWELL	SANTA FE	SILVER CITY	SOCORRO	TAOS	TUCUMCARI
ALBUQUERQUE	213		275	220	263	181	141	316	220	115	92	221	199	55	234	77	123	174
FARMINGTON	399	181	455	401	450		120	496	407	264	196	300	379	205	361	263	211	355
LAS CRUCES	65	220	203	293	42	407	338	250		335	312	441	182	275	111	146	343	394
ROSWELL	117	199	76	110	203	379	340	117	182	178	228	284		191	293	164	248	161
SANTA FE	220	55	267	213	319	205	197	308	275	65	37	171	191		290	132	68	167

DRIVING DISTANCES IN MILES

SEE ALSO MILEAGE AND DRIVING TIME MAP ON PAGES 6–7

© MapQuest.com, Inc.

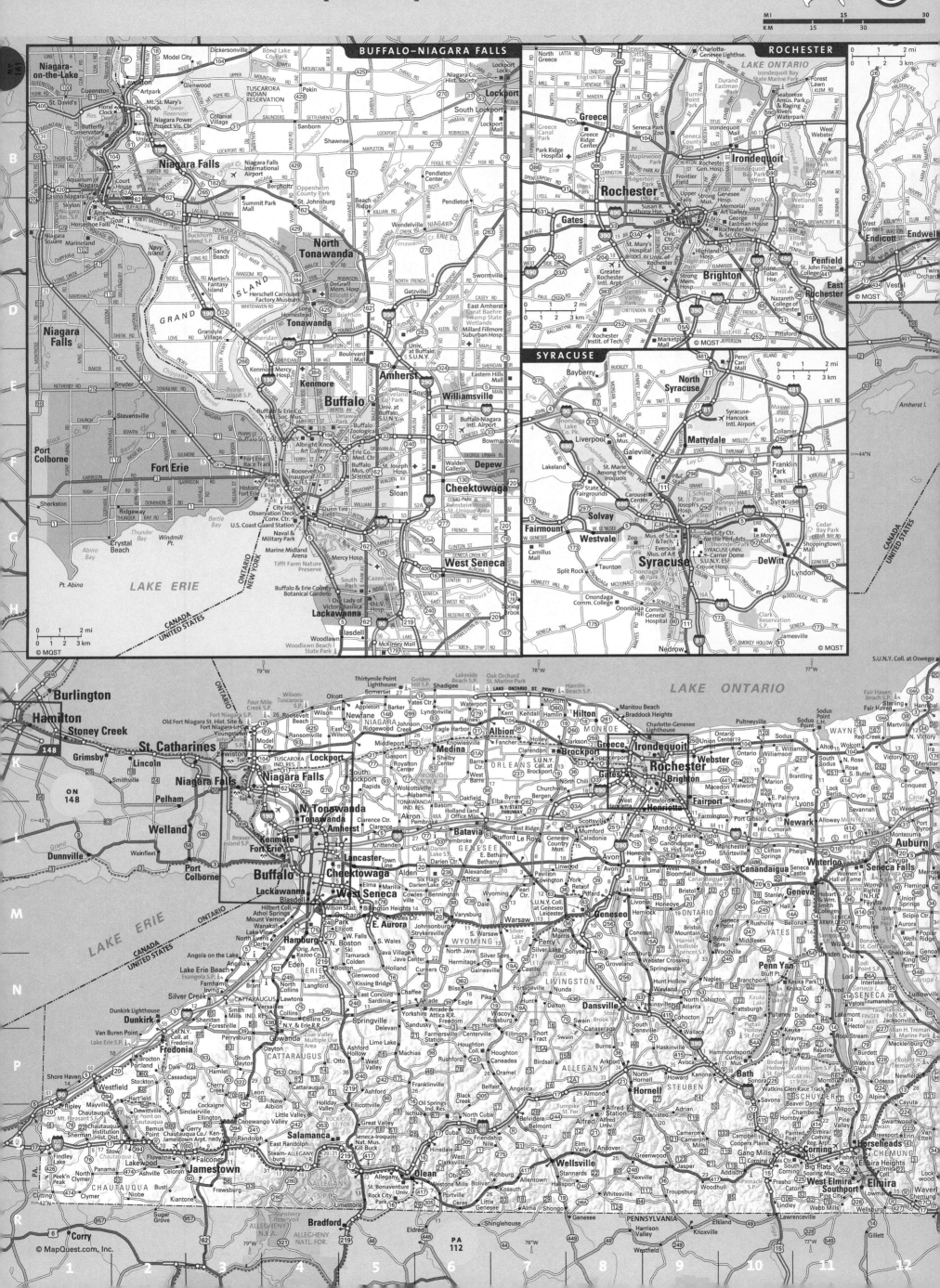

DRIVING DISTANCES IN MILES

	ALBANY	BINGHAMTON	BUFFALO	COOPERSTOWN	GENEVA	ITHACA	JAMESTOWN	KINGSTON	LAKE PLACID	NEW YORK	NIAGARA FALLS	OLEAN	PLATTSBURGH	ROCHESTER	SARATOGA SPRINGS	SYRACUSE	UTICA	WATERTOWN
ALBANY		135	292	89	197	186	361	56	138	151	306	297	160	228	32	146	94	179
BINGHAMTON	135		225	78	97	53	214	125	253	176	239	164	276	161	160	76	95	139
BUFFALO	292	225		239	103	153	74	346	337	400	20	74	374	74	293	152	199	210
ROCHESTER	228	161	74	175	39	89	142	282	273	336	88	113	310		229	88	135	146
SYRACUSE	146	76	152	93	56	59	220	201	192	250	166	163	228	88	147		53	65

SEE ALSO MILEAGE AND DRIVING TIME MAP ON PAGES 6–7

	ALBANY	BINGHAMTON	BUFFALO	HEMPSTEAD	KINGSTON	MIDDLETOWN	MONTAUK	MONTICELLO	NEWBURGH	NEW YORK	PEEKSKILL	PORT JEFFERSON	PORT JERVIS	POUGHKEEPSIE	RIVERHEAD	ROCHESTER	SYRACUSE	WHITE PLAINS
ALBANY		135	292	182	56	105	276	103	89	151	107	214	121	79	234	228	150	148
BINGHAMTON	135		225	203	125	116	296	87	134	176	144	235	117	127	254	161	76	167
KINGSTON	56	125	346	132		55	225	53	39	101	57	164	71	20	183	282	201	98
NEWBURGH	89	134	357	74	39	26	167	47		56	18	106	42	22	125	294	208	42
NEW YORK	151	176	400	26	101	72	120	95	56		45	58	87	96	78	336	250	29

DRIVING DISTANCES IN MILES

SEE ALSO MILEAGE AND DRIVING TIME MAP ON PAGES 6–7

© MapQuest.com, Inc.

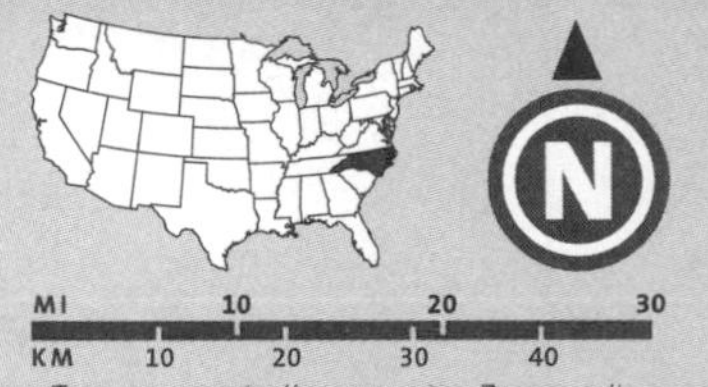

MI 10 20 30
KM 10 20 30 40

WESTERN NORTH CAROLINA

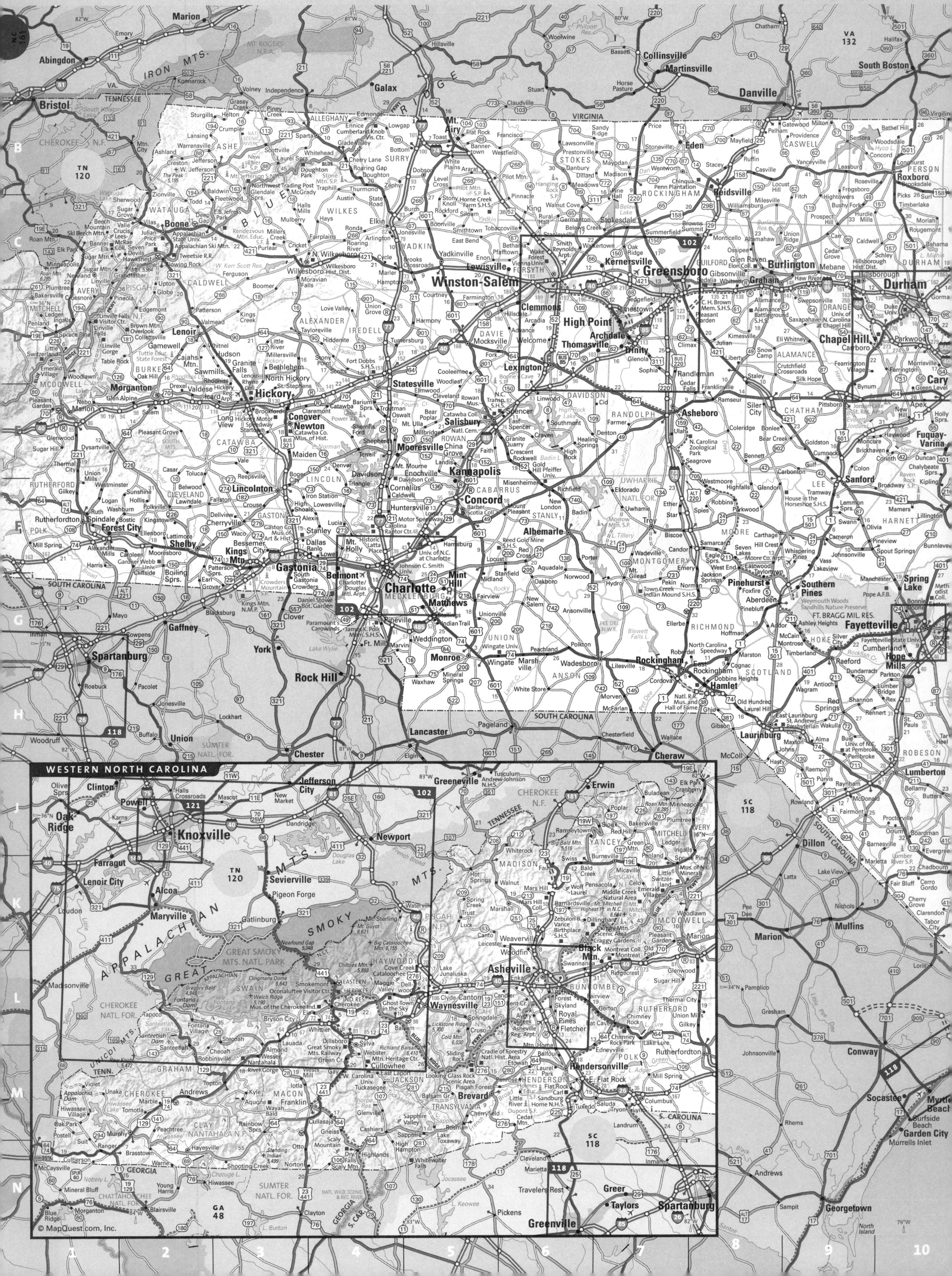

Major cities and places (map labels):

Bristol, Abingdon, Marion, Collinsville, Martinsville, Danville, South Boston, Halifax

Boone, Galax, Mt. Airy, Eden, Reidsville, Roxboro

Winston-Salem, Greensboro, Burlington, Graham, Durham, Chapel Hill, Cary

Hickory, Statesville, Salisbury, Lexington, High Point, Thomasville, Asheboro, Sanford, Siler City

Morganton, Lenoir, Mooresville, Kannapolis, Concord, Albemarle, Troy, Carthage, Pinehurst, Southern Pines, Aberdeen

Forest City, Shelby, Kings Mtn., Gastonia, Belmont, Charlotte, Matthews, Mint Hill, Monroe, Wadesboro, Rockingham, Hamlet, Laurinburg, Fayetteville, Hope Mills, Spring Lake

Spartanburg, Gaffney, York, Rock Hill, Lancaster, Cheraw, Lumberton, Dillon

Knoxville, Sevierville, Pigeon Forge, Gatlinburg, Maryville, Alcoa, Lenoir City, Loudon, Newport, Jefferson City, Greeneville, Erwin

Great Smoky Mts. Natl. Park, Appalachian Mts., Cherokee, Bryson City, Franklin, Waynesville, Asheville, Black Mtn., Hendersonville, Brevard, Marion

Murphy, Andrews, Robbinsville

Greenville, Greer, Taylors, Socastee, Myrtle Beach, Garden City, Georgetown, Conway

© MapQuest.com, Inc.

	ASHEVILLE	BOONE	CHARLOTTE	DURHAM	ELIZABETH CITY	FAYETTEVILLE	GREENSBORO	GREENVILLE	HICKORY	JACKSONVILLE	KINSTON	MOREHEAD CITY	NAGS HEAD	RALEIGH	ROCKINGHAM	ROCKY MOUNT	WILMINGTON	WINSTON-SALEM
ASHEVILLE		198	116	224	404	264	176	324	78	354	316	383	444	242	190	297	368	146
CHARLOTTE	116	95		139	319	139	91	239	48	269	232	298	359	158	74	213	205	79
GREENSBORO	176	117	91		228	90		148	98	179	141	207	268	67	83	122	193	30
RALEIGH	242	183	158	24	160	62	67	80	164	113	76	142	200		96	54	127	96
WILMINGTON	368	309	205	150	211	92	193	130	290	52	93	95	241	127	131	153		222

DRIVING DISTANCES IN MILES   SEE ALSO MILEAGE AND DRIVING TIME MAP ON PAGES 6–7

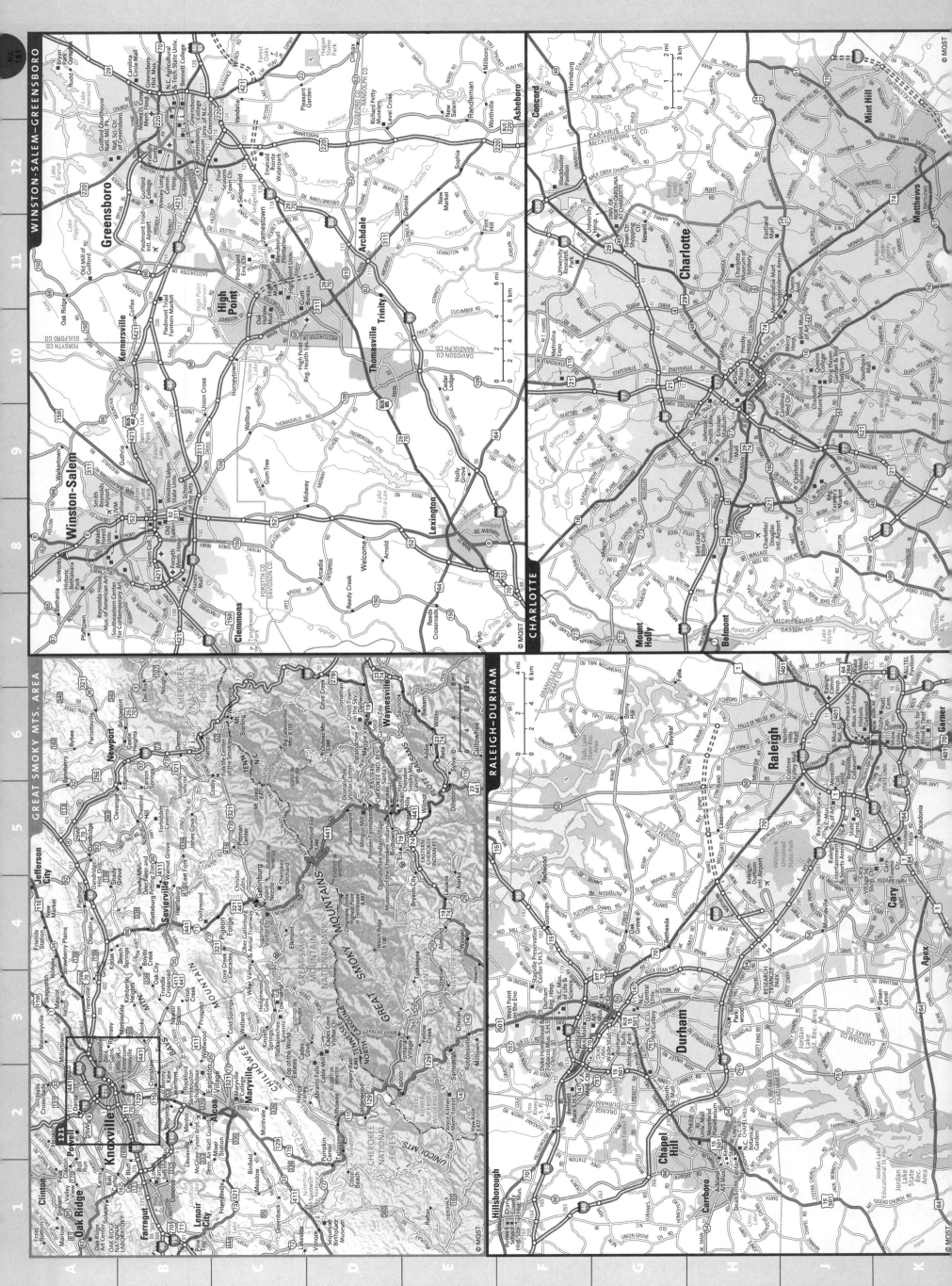

	BISMARCK	DICKINSON	FARGO	GRAND FORKS	JAMESTOWN	MINOT	PEMBINA	RUGBY	VALLEY CITY	WAHPETON	WILLISTON
BISMARCK		186	97	199	274	105	116	347	153	141	249	229
DICKINSON	97		278	291	367	197	178	440	245	234	341	133
FARGO	199	163		291	79	97	268	152	221	58	55	424
GRAND FORKS	274	91	367		79	173	212	77	148	133	130	340
MINOT	116	122	178	268		212	171		238	64	210	318	128

DRIVING DISTANCES IN MILES

SEE ALSO MILEAGE AND DRIVING TIME MAP ON PAGES 6–7

© MapQuest.com, Inc.

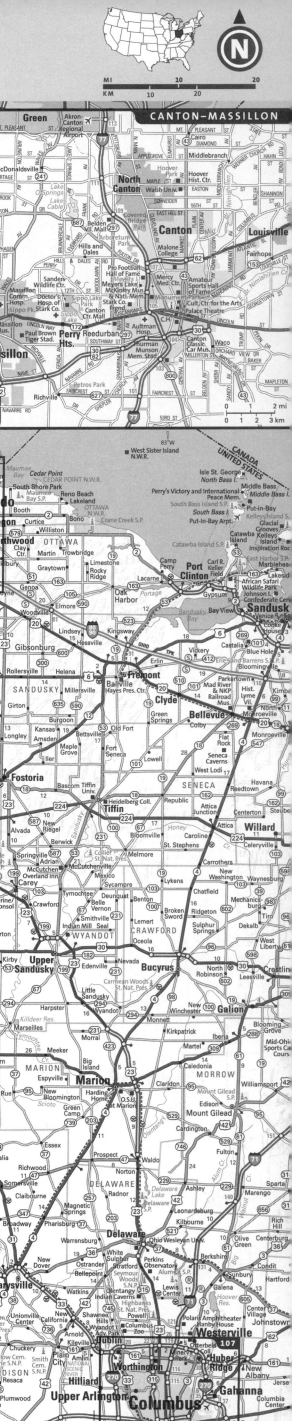

	AKRON	CAMBRIDGE	CHILLICOTHE	CINCINNATI	CLEVELAND	COLUMBUS	DAYTON	DEFIANCE	FINDLAY	LIMA	MANSFIELD	MARION	NEW PHILADELPHIA	SANDUSKY	SPRINGFIELD	TOLEDO	YOUNGSTOWN
AKRON		83	23	184	243	38	129	198	186	140	157	66	101	46	84	172	142	49
CAMBRIDGE	83		61	98	187	124	80	155	228	178	175	108	126	37	169	128	228	129
CLEVELAND	38	124	64	199	259		144	213	163	126	163	81	116	87	61	187	119	75
COLUMBUS	129	80	143	47	110	144		70	146	101	96	67	50	117	119	44	148	179
TOLEDO	142	228	168	189	209	119	148	156	63	51	83	105	100	191	62	169		179

DRIVING DISTANCES IN MILES   SEE ALSO MILEAGE AND DRIVING TIME MAP ON PAGES 6–7

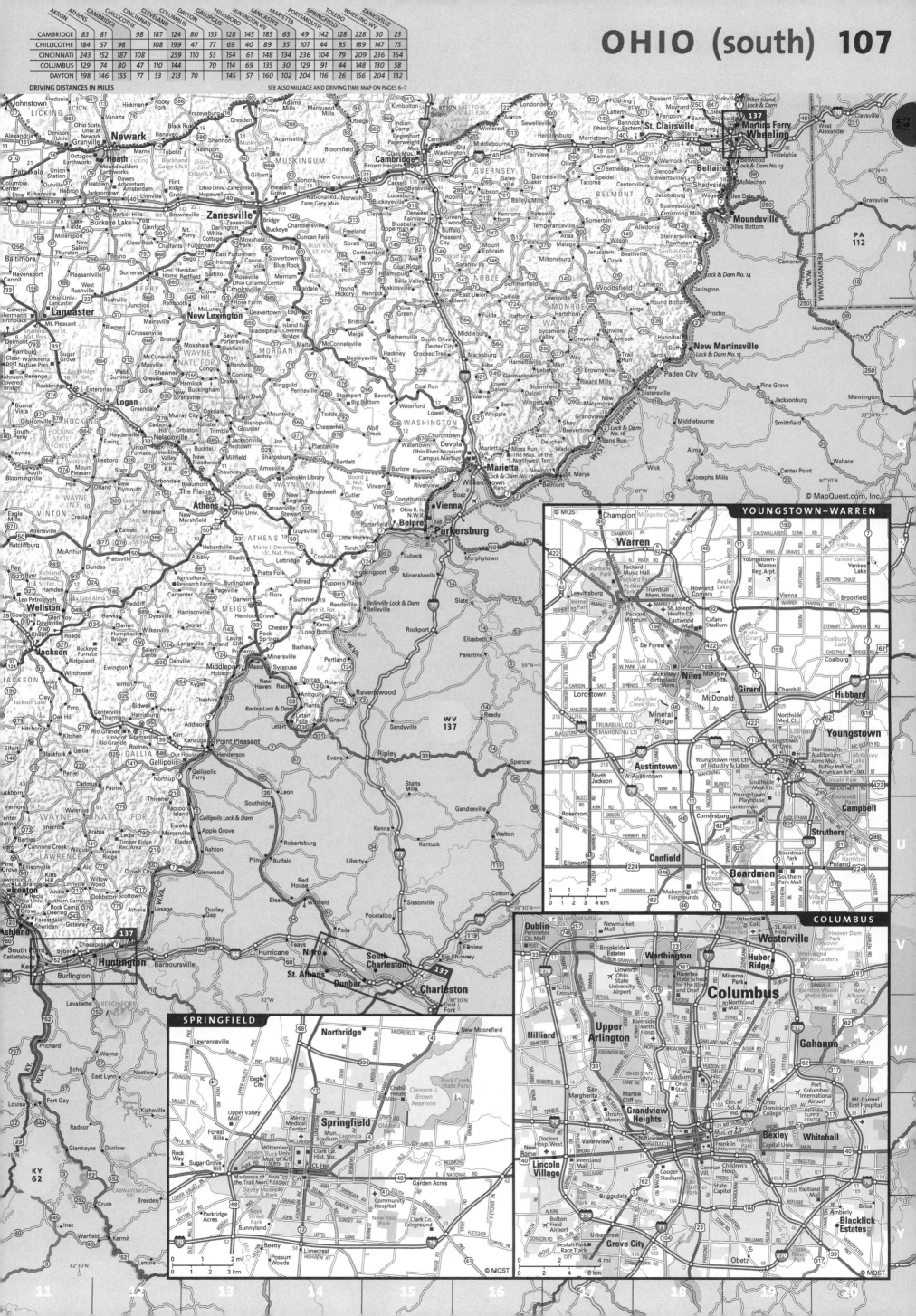

DRIVING DISTANCES IN MILES

	AKRON	ATHENS	CAMBRIDGE	CHILLICOTHE	CINCINNATI	CLEVELAND	COLUMBUS	DAYTON	GALLIPOLIS	HILLSBORO	HUNTINGTON WV	LANCASTER	MARIETTA	PORTSMOUTH	SPRINGFIELD	TOLEDO	WHEELING WV	ZANESVILLE
CAMBRIDGE	83	81		98	187	124	80	155	128	185	63	49	142	128	228	50	23	
CHILLICOTHE	184	57	98		108	199	47	77	69	40	89	35	107	44	85	189	147	75
CINCINNATI	243	152	187	108		259	104	53	154	61	148	134	236	104	79	209	236	164
COLUMBUS	129	74	80	47	110	144		70	114	69	135	30	129	91	44	148	130	58
DAYTON	198	146	155	77	53	213	70		145	57	160	102	204	116	26	156	204	132

SEE ALSO MILEAGE AND DRIVING TIME MAP ON PAGES 6–7

© MapQuest.com, Inc.

YOUNGSTOWN–WARREN

COLUMBUS

SPRINGFIELD

	ARDMORE	BARTLESVILLE	DALLAS, TX	DURANT	ELK CITY	ENID	FORT SMITH, AR	GUYMON	HUGO	LAWTON	MC ALESTER	MIAMI	MUSKOGEE	OKLAHOMA CITY	PONCA CITY	STILLWATER	TULSA	WOODWARD
ENID	183	141	292	238	148		242	219	282	142	210	207	168	84	69	66	117	88
LAWTON	103	243	197	158	115	142	270	297	224		211	283	223	85	192	152	194	175
MC ALESTER	117	141	169	77	245	210	114	407	75	211		160	68	133	186	154	93	276
OKLAHOMA CITY	99	157	209	164	112	84	191	274	205	85	133	198	144		107	67	109	143
TULSA	206	48	259	168	221	117	125	336	165	194	93	91	52	109	93	71		205

DRIVING DISTANCES IN MILES   SEE ALSO MILEAGE AND DRIVING TIME MAP ON PAGES 6–7

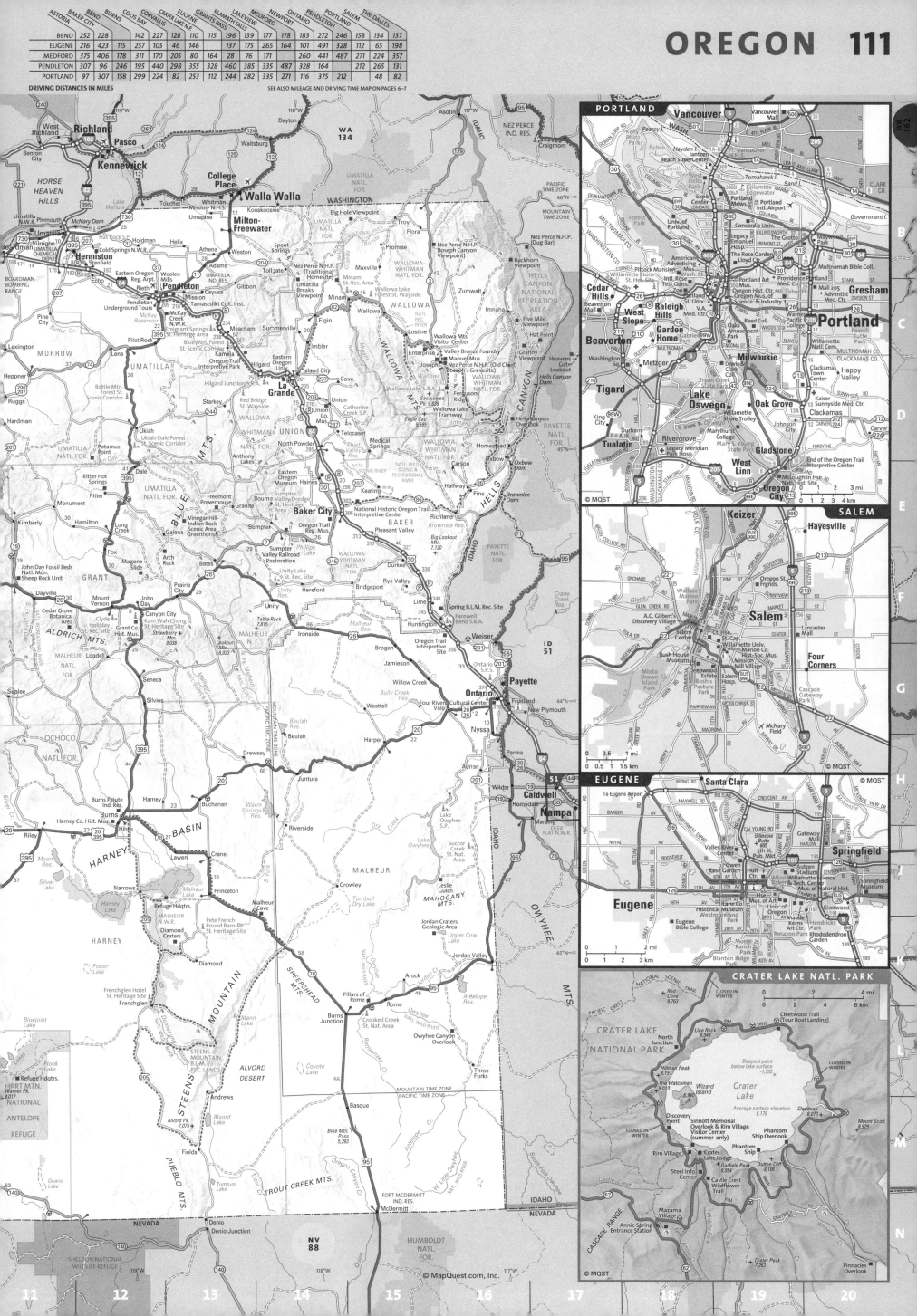

	ALLENTOWN	ALTOONA	CHAMBERSBURG	EAST STROUDSBURG	ERIE	GETTYSBURG	HARRISBURG	LANCASTER	LEWISTOWN	PHILADELPHIA	PITTSBURGH	READING	SCRANTON	STATE COLLEGE	SUNBURY	WILKES-BARRE	WILLIAMSPORT	YORK
ALLENTOWN		218	133	39	361	125	82	71	137	63	284	37	76	165	93	64	116	91
HARRISBURG	82	140	54	121	298	42		44	58	109	205	65	109	88	52	105	83	25
PHILADELPHIA	63	241	154	87	405	131	109	79	164		306	63	128	195	144	117	169	100
SCRANTON	76	185	170	50	317	162	119	130	128	301	103	149		84	17	83	143	
WILLIAMSPORT	116	99	134	118	259	125	83	124	83	169	215	103	83	63	34	66		108

DRIVING DISTANCES IN MILES

SEE ALSO MILEAGE AND DRIVING TIME MAP ON PAGES 6–7

	CHARLESTON	CHARLOTTE, NC	COLUMBIA	FLORENCE	GREENVILLE	HILTON HEAD ISLAND	MYRTLE BEACH	ROCK HILL	SAVANNAH, GA	SPARTANBURG	SUMTER
AUGUSTA, GA											
CHARLESTON	142	204		110	127	205	95	92	183	107	200	100
COLUMBIA	70	91	110		80	97	152	146	70	159	92	45
FLORENCE	147	107	127	80		174	170	66	115	176	169	39
GREENVILLE	110	96	205	97	174		248	241	88	255	30	142
MYRTLE BEACH	213	173	92	146	66	241	190		181	197	235	93

DRIVING DISTANCES IN MILES   SEE ALSO MILEAGE AND DRIVING TIME MAP ON PAGES 6–7

DRIVING DISTANCES IN MILES

SEE ALSO MILEAGE AND DRIVING TIME MAP ON PAGES 6–7

	ABERDEEN	BELLE FOURCHE	BROOKINGS	HOT SPRINGS	HURON	MITCHELL	MOBRIDGE	PIERRE	RAPID CITY	SIOUX FALLS	WATERTOWN	YANKTON
ABERDEEN		310	150	412	90	146	99	160	357	204	98	231
PIERRE	160	247	188	247	115	155	107		193	226	189	240
RAPID CITY	357	56	390	56	313	275	243	193		346	436	360
SIOUX FALLS	204	401	57	401	127	73	303	226	346		103	80
WATERTOWN	98	360	49	490	86	162	196	189	436	103		179

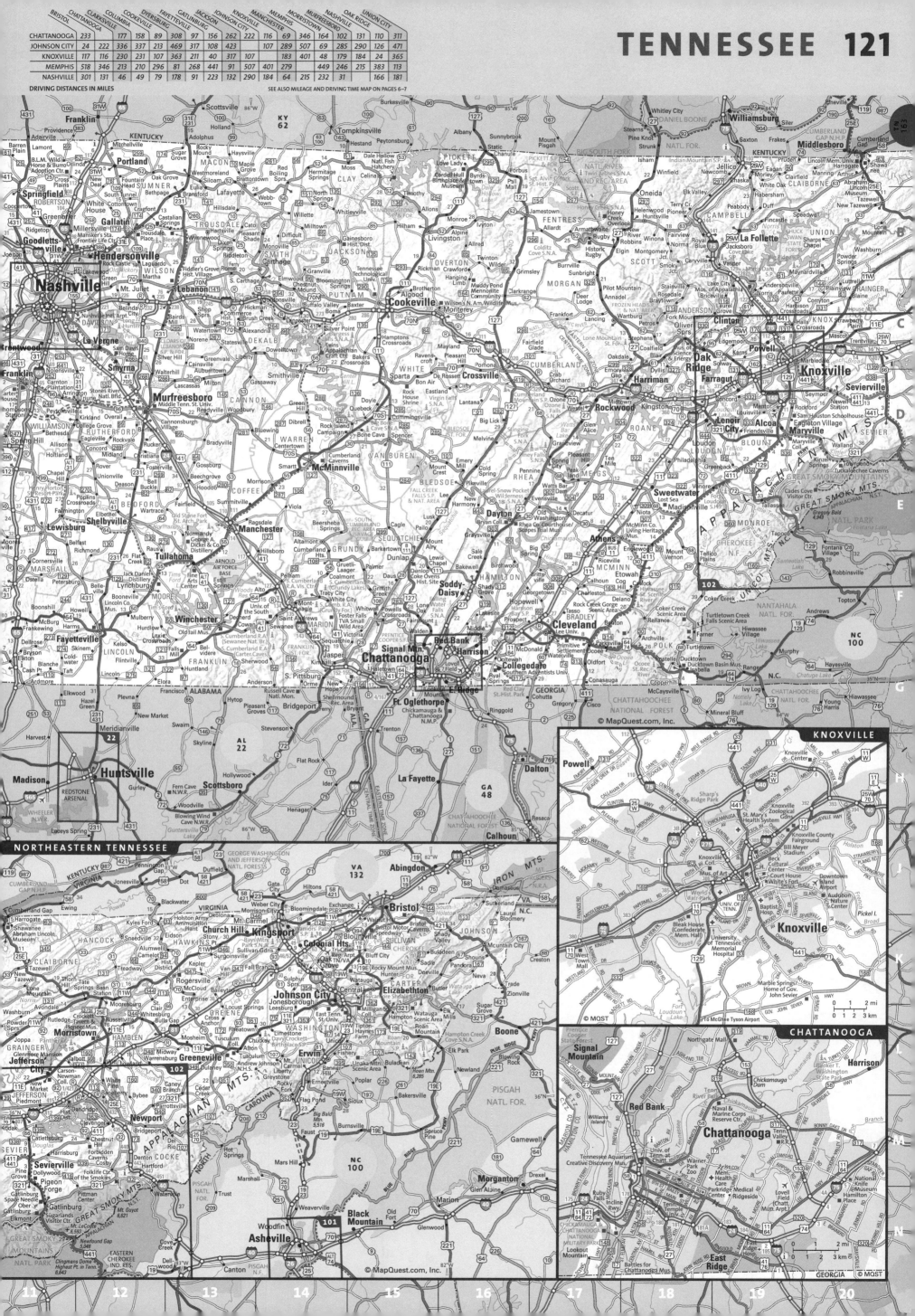

	BRISTOL	CHATTANOOGA	CLARKSVILLE	COLUMBIA	COOKEVILLE	DYERSBURG	FAYETTEVILLE	GATLINBURG	JACKSON	JOHNSON CITY	KNOXVILLE	MANCHESTER	MEMPHIS	MORRISTOWN	MURFREESBORO	NASHVILLE	OAK RIDGE	UNION CITY
CHATTANOOGA	233		177	158	89	308	97	156	262	222	116	69	346	54	102	131	110	311
JOHNSON CITY	24	222	336	337	213	469	317	108	423		108	289	507	69	285	290	126	471
KNOXVILLE	117	116	230	231	107	363	211	40	317	107		183	401	48	179	184	24	365
MEMPHIS	518	346	213	210	296	81	268	441	91	507	401	279		449	246	215	383	113
NASHVILLE	301	131	46	49	79	178	91	223	132	290	184	64	215	232	31		166	181

DRIVING DISTANCES IN MILES   SEE ALSO MILEAGE AND DRIVING TIME MAP ON PAGES 6–7

NORTHEASTERN TENNESSEE

KNOXVILLE

CHATTANOOGA

© MapQuest.com, Inc.

| 11 | 12 | 13 | 14 | 15 | 16 | 17 | 18 | 19 | 20 |

DRIVING DISTANCES IN MILES   SEE ALSO MILEAGE AND DRIVING TIME MAP ON PAGES 6-7

	ABILENE	ALPINE	AMARILLO	BIG BEND N.P.	BIG SPRING	CHILDRESS	DALHART	DALLAS	DEL RIO	EL PASO	FORT STOCKTON	LUBBOCK	ODESSA	PECOS	SAN ANGELO	SAN ANTONIO	VAN HORN	WICHITA FALLS
AMARILLO	290	414		472	230	118	87	470	462	438	349	124	266	340	308	513	427	228
EL PASO	459	232	438	329	347	558	420	647	425		241	341	285	209	416	556	122	596
LUBBOCK	166	291	124	349	106	144	211	354	338	341	226		142	217	185	389	303	207
ODESSA	176	151	266	209	65	276	353	364	246	285	86	142		76	134	342	163	314
SAN ANGELO	91	230	308	287	87	238	395	265	156	416	164	185	134	208		208	295	232

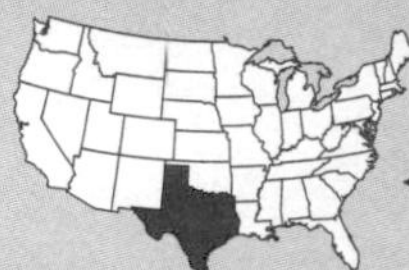

MI 0 25 50
KM 25 50

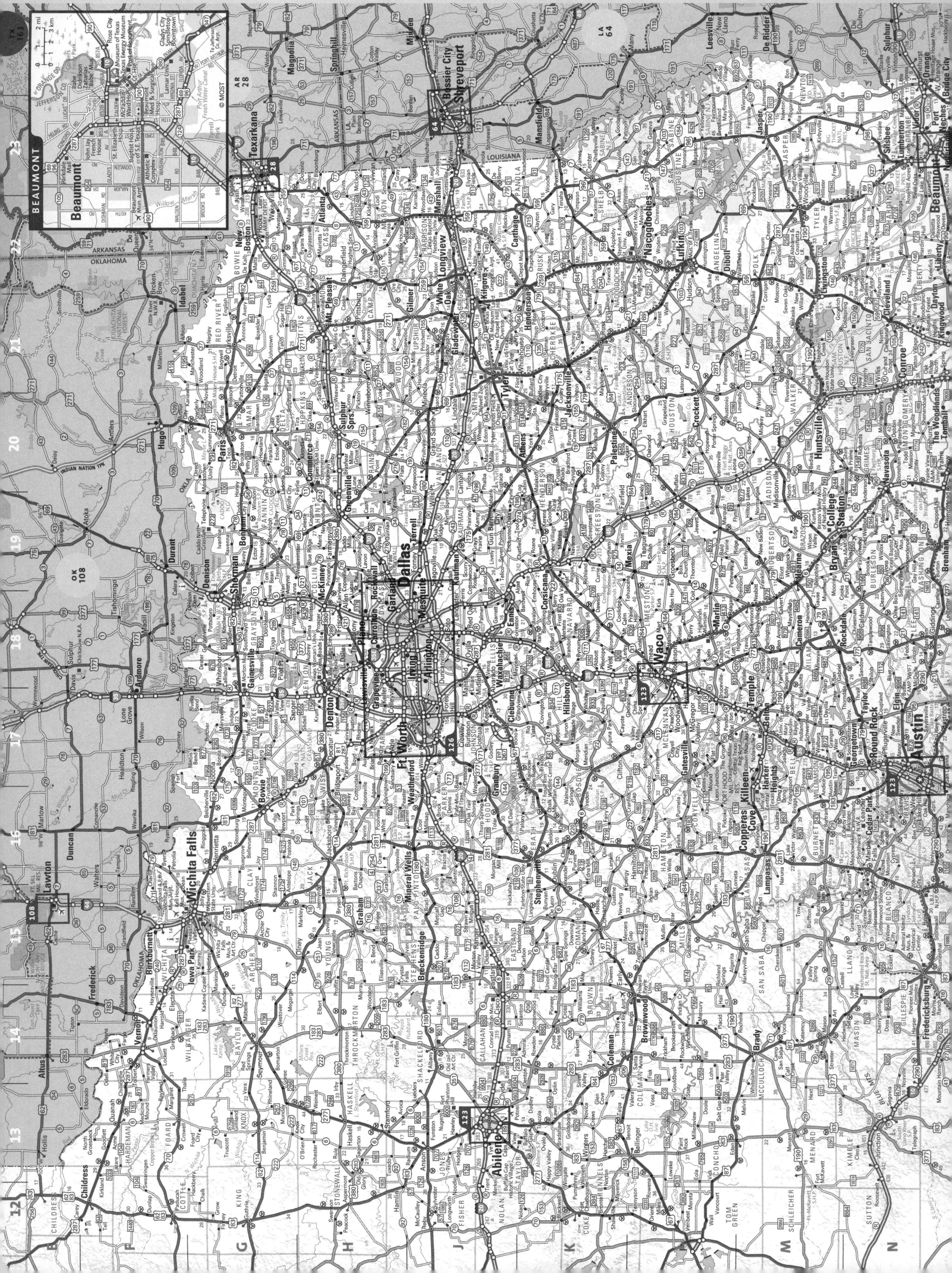

DRIVING DISTANCES IN MILES

SEE ALSO MILEAGE AND DRIVING TIME MAP ON PAGES 6–7

	ABILENE	AUSTIN	BEAUMONT	BROWNSVILLE	COLLEGE STATION	CORPUS CHRISTI	DALLAS	DEL RIO	FORT WORTH	HOUSTON	LAREDO	MC ALLEN	SAN ANGELO	SAN ANTONIO	TEXARKANA	TYLER	WACO	WICHITA FALLS
AUSTIN	217		250	350	108	217	190	187	166	238	313	229	207	78	375	229	105	301
CORPUS CHRISTI	411	217	293	157	254		411	272	403	211	141	152	362	147	591	445	321	517
DALLAS	191	195	323	544	184	411		422	32	241	432	507	265	271	179	100	94	141
HOUSTON	425	166	84	351	106	211	241	349		355	346	410	200	290	202	203	382
SAN ANTONIO	258	78	284	279	171	147	271	152	264	200	157	243	208		452	306	182	378

DOWNTOWN SAN ANTONIO

CORPUS CHRISTI

SAN ANTONIO

LAREDO

© MapQuest.com, Inc.

DISTANCES BETWEEN CITIES ARE COMPUTED IN KILOMETERS OVER MAIN HIGHWAYS AND INCLUDE FERRY DISTANCES

Distance chart — origin cities (read along the diagonal):

- BAIE-COMEAU, QC
- BANFF, AB
- BOSTON, MA
- BRANDON, MB
- CALGARY, AB
- CHARLOTTETOWN, PE
- CHICAGO, IL
- DAWSON CREEK, BC
- EDMONTON, AB
- FREDERICTON, NB
- HALIFAX, NS
- KENORA, ON
- MINNEAPOLIS, MN
- MONTRÉAL, QC
- NEW YORK, NY
- NORTH BAY, ON
- OTTAWA, ON
- PRINCE GEORGE, BC
- PRINCE RUPERT, BC
- QUÉBEC, QC
- REGINA, SK
- SAINT JOHN, NB
- ST. JOHN'S, NF
- SASKATOON, SK
- SAULT STE. MARIE, ON
- SEATTLE, WA
- SYDNEY, NS
- THUNDER BAY, ON
- TORONTO, ON
- VANCOUVER, BC
- VICTORIA, BC
- WHITEHORSE, YT
- WINDSOR, ON
- WINNIPEG, MB
- YELLOWKNIFE, NT

Distance values (by origin row):

Baie-Comeau, QC	4234 978 3019 4117 735 1947 4749 4152 600 856 2586 2614 663 1189 769 4894 5579 400 3376 689 3639 1563 5274 1072 2136 1127 5489 5570 6067 1490 2792 5578
Banff, AB	4434 1234 128 4681 2811 1001 412 4432 4802 1648 2156 4104 3137 3500 637 1323 3888 856 4521 6032 729 2725 977 5018 2105 3642 819 874 2219 3280 1429 1830
Boston, MA	3220 4318 1049 1614 4950 4353 690 1149 2639 2280 504 346 1036 665 5093 5779 634 3577 779 2379 3840 1572 4941 1365 2187 917 5156 5255 6268 1181 3006 5779
Brandon, MB	1117 3468 1598 1749 1152 3217 3589 434 943 2438 2889 1923 2287 1894 2580 2675 377 3306 4817 639 1510 2041 3804 892 2427 2016 2108 3067 2066 216 2578
Calgary, AB	4566 2696 885 296 4315 4686 1530 2041 3536 3986 3021 3384 755 1440 3772 740 4403 5914 613 2607 1093 4902 1989 3524 900 991 2203 3162 1313 1712
Charlottetown, PE	2382 5198 4601 354 322 3035 3048 1381 1574 1204 5341 6027 819 3825 312 1376 4088 1997 5708 374 2583 1561 5924 6003 6516 1925 3241 6027
Chicago, IL	3328 2731 2134 2504 1577 658 1353 1283 1138 1252 3471 4157 1604 1955 2222 2216 896 3318 2720 1521 821 3534 3613 4646 460 1384 4157
Dawson Creek, BC	597 4947 5319 2165 2673 4168 4620 3653 4017 406 1006 4405 1373 5035 6548 1132 3337 1283 5534 6542 7199 2704 4158 6542
Edmonton, AB	4350 4722 1566 2076 3571 4022 3056 3420 740 1426 3806 776 4438 5950 513 2642 1308 4937 2024 3560 1115 1207 1915 3198 1347 1426
Fredericton, NB	452 2784 2797 769 1022 1323 953 5092 5777 568 2334 105 1688 3837 1746 5457 689 2333 1310 5673 5752 6265 1674 2990 5776
Halifax, NS	3156 3169 1151 1481 1695 1324 5462 6148 940 3946 410 1402 4208 1811 5829 415 2704 1682 6045 6123 6148 2045 3362 6148
Kenora, ON	668 2005 2622 1489 1854 2308 2993 2240 792 2873 4384 1052 1077 2456 3371 459 1814 2432 2522 3483 1640 208 2992
Minneapolis, MN	2020 1949 1802 1918 2816 3502 2271 1299 2887 4398 1561 1173 2662 3386 547 1487 2877 2956 3989 1125 727 3069
Montréal, QC	616 544 194 4311 4997 250 2795 867 2379 3508 967 4678 1366 1553 531 4824 4905 5486 895 2211 4997
New York, NY	999 703 4764 5449 838 3248 1110 2710 3508 1545 4609 1696 2171 816 4825 4905 5938 1001 2675 5447
North Bay, ON	364 3796 4462 795 2280 1411 2924 2541 423 4146 1299 2887 3386 547 4877 4956 5447
Ottawa, ON	4160 4846 444 2644 1041 2552 2906 787 4578 1540 1401 431 4792 4873 5335 793 2060 4846
Prince George, BC	724 4548 5516 690 2379 941 5092 5777 568 4578 1255 3384 922 5678 2765 4302 778 821 1580 3940 2089 1553
Prince Rupert, BC	5233 2202 5864 7377 1941 4070 1608 6363 3450 4987 1502 1506 1315 4625 2774 2198
Québec, QC	3032 657 2168 3293 1218 4929 1155 1790 782 5143 5224 5723 1144 2448 5232
Regina, SK	3663 5176 261 1868 1664 4162 1761 2786 1640 1732 2691 2424 573 2202
Saint John, NB	1633 3925 1835 5546 647 2422 1398 5761 5840 6354 1762 3079 5864
St. John's, NF	5436 7058 1038 3933 2910 7272 7272 7866 3273 4590 7395
Saskatoon, SK	2129 1823 4424 1511 3046 1630 1722 2430 2684 834 1939
Sault Ste. Marie, ON	4223 2333 649 674 3508 3598 4559 563 1283 4068
Seattle, WA	6048 2913 4147 225 177 2504 3787 2237 2475
Sydney, NS	2919 1897 6240 6339 6852 2261 3577 6363
Thunder Bay, ON	1355 2889 2980 3940 1699 665 3455
Toronto, ON	4363 4443 5476 364 2213 4986
Vancouver, BC	93 2311 4001 2213 2282
Victoria, BC	2401 4081 2305 2374
Whitehorse, YT	5114 3264 1846
Windsor, ON	1852 4624
Winnipeg, MB	2773

© MQST

© MapQuest.com, Inc.

	CRANBROOK	DAWSON CREEK	JASPER, AB	KAMLOOPS	KELOWNA	NANAIMO	PRINCE GEORGE	PRINCE RUPERT	REVELSTOKE	VANCOUVER	VICTORIA
CRANBROOK		265	985	504	600	513	845*	838	1562	196	765	882*
KAMLOOPS	479	600	931	444		163	359*	525	1249	206	340	396*
KELOWNA	476	513	1094	597	163		383*	688	1409	192	378	420*
PRINCE GEORGE	637	838	406	376	525	688	784*		724	693	778	821*
VANCOUVER	819	765	1184	374	340	378	109*	778	1502	546		93*

DRIVING DISTANCES IN KILOMETERS
*DISTANCE INCLUDES FERRY TRAVEL

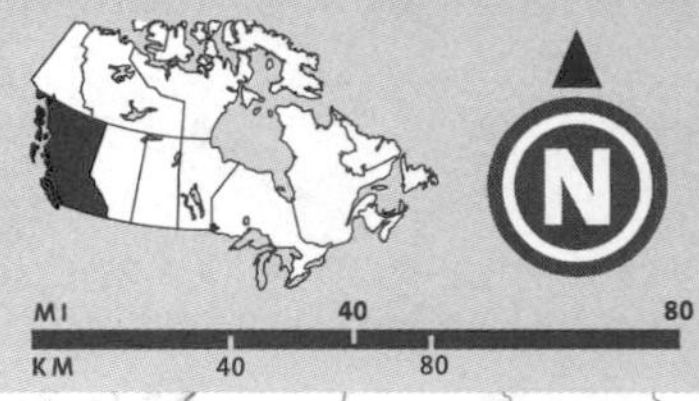

VANCOUVER

VICTORIA

PACIFIC OCEAN

DISTANCES IN CANADA SHOWN IN KILOMETERS

© MapQuest.com, Inc.

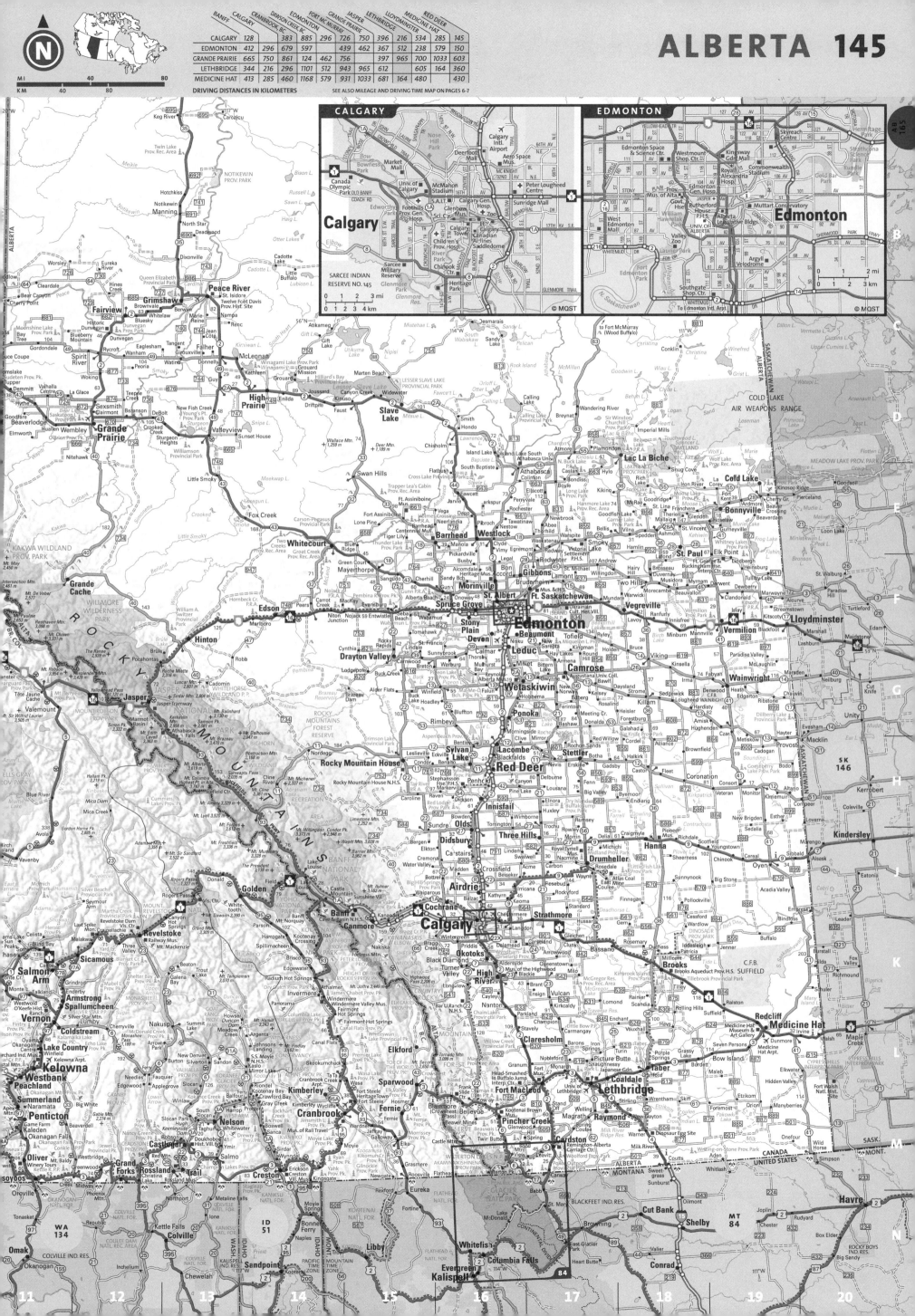

	BANFF	CALGARY	CRANBROOK, BC	DAWSON CREEK, BC	EDMONTON	FORT MC MURRAY	GRANDE PRAIRIE	JASPER	LETHBRIDGE	LLOYDMINSTER	MEDICINE HAT	RED DEER
CALGARY	128		383	885	296	726	750	396	216	534	285	145
EDMONTON	412	296	679	597		439	462	367	512	238	579	150
GRANDE PRAIRIE	665	750	861	124	462	756		397	965	700	1033	603
LETHBRIDGE	344	216	296	1101	512	943	965	612		605	164	360
MEDICINE HAT	413	285	460	1168	579	931	1033	681	164	480		430

DRIVING DISTANCES IN KILOMETERS   SEE ALSO MILEAGE AND DRIVING TIME MAP ON PAGES 6-7

CALGARY

Calgary

SARCEE INDIAN
RESERVE NO. 145

EDMONTON

Edmonton

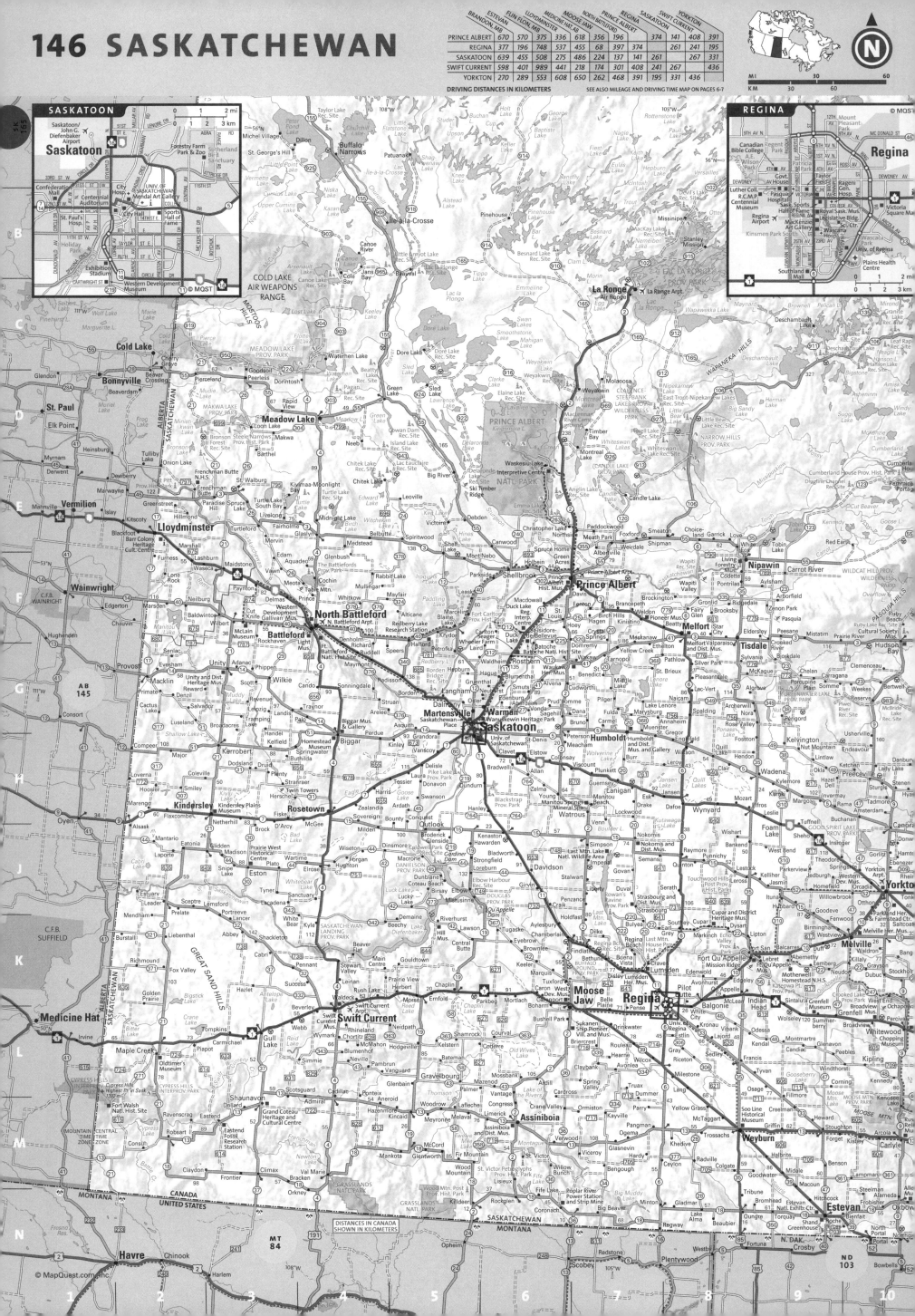

MI
20 40
KM
20 40

ON 147

DISTANCES IN CANADA
SHOWN IN KILOMETERS

HAMILTON

0   1   2 mi
0   1   2   3 km

Flamborough

Burlington

Royal Botanical Gardens

Hamilton

LAKE
ONTARIO

Dundas

Hamilton

Ancaster

Stoney
Creek

Hamilton Intl. Airport

LONDON

0   1   2 mi
0   1   2   3 km

London Airport

London

MI
74

Port Huron

Sarnia

Marysville

St. Clair

LAKE
HURON

Georgian
Bay

Bruce
Peninsula

Owen Sound

Collingwood

Wasaga
Beach

Penetanguishene

Midland

Barr

Kincardine

Hanover

Durham

Orangeville

Bolton

Brampton

Goderich

Listowel

Fergus

Elmira

Brampton

Clinton

Guelph

Mississauga

Waterloo

Kitchener

Oakville

Stratford

Cambridge

Burlington

Hamilton

St. Marys

Paris

Dundas
Ancaster

Stoney
Creek

Grims

Woodstock

Brantford

Lansing

Ingersoll

London

Strathroy

St.
Thomas

Aylmer

Tillsonburg

Simco

Port Dover

Long Point
Bay

Pontiac

Sterling Hts.

Warren

New
Baltimore

Wallaceburg

Chatham (Chatham-Kent)

Detroit

Windsor

Dearborn

LAKE
ST. CLAIR

Ann Arbor

Taylor

Amherstburg

Harrow

Kingsville

Leamington

LAKE
ERIE

Erie

TRAVEL NOTE: Reclassification of Ontario
roads at time of publication may result in
highway number changes.

© MQST

	BARRIE	HAMILTON	KENORA	KINGSTON	KITCHENER	LONDON	NIAGARA FALLS	NORTH BAY	OTTAWA	OWEN SOUND	PETERBOROUGH	SARNIA	SAULT STE MARIE	SUDBURY	THUNDER BAY	TIMMINS	TORONTO	WINDSOR
LONDON	248	134	1926	434	105		227	499	613	208	309	109	818	1467	840	183	195
OTTAWA	442	504	1854	179	496	613	574	364		558	265	714	787	488	1401	705	431	793
SUDBURY	319	462	1407	600	453	570	533	124	488	435	404	673	299		948	290	407	751
THUNDER BAY	1219	1410	459	1548	1401	1467	1481	1072	1335	1371	1621	649	948		1355	1355	1699
TORONTO	105	74	1814	251	104	183	145	336	431	183	127	285	674	407	1355	677		364

DRIVING DISTANCES IN KILOMETERS   SEE ALSO MILEAGE AND DRIVING TIME MAP ON PAGES 6-7

SUDBURY

DOWNTOWN TORONTO

© MapQuest.com, Inc.

© MQST

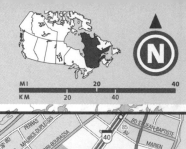

MI 20 40
KM 20 40

MONTRÉAL

Montréal-Est
Îles-de-Boucherville
Anjou
Montréal-Nord
Laval
St-Léonard
Longueuil
Montréal
St-Léonard
Outremont
St-Lambert
St-Laurent
Mont-Royal
St-Hubert
Hampstead
Côte-St-Luc
Westmount
Greenfield Park
Lachine
Montréal St-Pierre
Dorval
Verdun
Brossard
Montréal International Airport-Dorval
LaSalle
Lac St-Louis
Bassin de Laprairie
Kahnawake
The Fur Trade at Lachine National Historic Site
© MQST
KAHNAWAKE IND. RES.
Sainte-Catherine
La Prairie

0 1 2 mi
0 1 2 3 km

Val-Paradis
Villebois
Normétal
Beaucanton
St-Lambert
Val-St-Gilles
La Reine
Chazel
St-Eugène-de-Chazel
Lébel-sur-Quévillon
Rapide-des-Cèdres
Dupuy
La Sarre
Clerval
Colombourg
Macamic
Authier-Nord
Languedoc
St-Gérard-de-Berry
Ste-Hélène-de-Mancebourg
Authier
St-Dominique-du-Rosaire
L'Île-Nepawa
Palmarolle
Poularies
Ste-Germaine-Boulé
Guyenne
St-Nazaire-de-Berry
Despinassy
Roquemaure
Gallichan
Laferté
Launay
Villemontel
Rochebaucourt
Rapide-Danseur
Taschereau
Amos
Landrienne
Champneuf
PARC D'AIGUEBELLE
Pikogan
St-Marc-de-Figuery
Barville
Le Morandière
Duparquet
Destor
St-Mathieu-d'Harricana
Vassan
Barraute
D'Alembert
St-Joseph-de-Cléricy
Vautrin
Preissac
La Corne
Belcourt
Rouyn-Noranda
Lac Preissac
Senneterre
Univ. du Québec en Abitibi-Témiscamingue
St-Norbert-de-Mont-Brun
Senneville
McWatters
Cadillac
La Motte
Évain
Granada
Rivière-Héva
Sullivan
Virginiatown
Beaudry
Mus. Rég. des Mines
Malartic
Val-Senpeville
Cloutier
Bellecombe
Dubuisson
Obaska
Montbeillard
St-Roch
Val-d'Or
Val-d'Or Arpt.
Louvicourt
Lac-Simon

RÉSERVE FAUNIQUE LA VÉRENDRYE

Témiscamingue
Notre-Dame-du-Nord
Angliers
Winneway
St-Bruno-de-Guigues
St-Eugène-de-Guigues
Moffet
Hailleybury
Laverlochère
Laforce
Latulipe
Ville-Marie
Lorrainville
Fugèreville
Belleterre
Fort Témiscamingue Natl. Hist. Site
Fabre
Béarn

ZEC NORMANDIE
Réservoir Mitchinamecus
Réservoir Cabonga
ZEC PETAWAGA
ZEC MAZANA
RÉS. FAUNIQUE ROUGE-MATAWIN
Ste-Anne-du-Lac
Mont-St-Michel
Poissant
ZEC DE LA MAISON DE PIERRE
ZEC KIPAWA
Hunter's Point
Kebaowek
Kipawa
Tee Lake
ZEC RESTIGO
ZEC BEAUCHÊNE
Grand-Remous
Val-Limoges
Chute-St-Philippe
Guénette
L'Ascension
North Bay
Mattawa
ZEC MAGANASIPI
Montcerf
Bois Franc
Mont-Laurier
Val-Barrette
Lac-Saguay
Ste-Véronique
Powassan
Maniwaki
Messines
Farley
Ste-Famille-d'Aumond
Lac-des-Îles
Kiamika
Lac Nominingue
L'Annonciation
La Macaza
DISTANCES IN CANADA SHOWN IN KILOMETERS
Déléage
Bellerive-sur-Lac
Mont-Tremblant
© MapQuest.com, Inc.
Rapides-des-Joachims
Bouchette
Notre-Dame-du-Laur
Gracefield
Blue Sea
Mont-Tremblant-Village
ALGONQUIN PROVINCIAL PARK
Deep River
Chalk River
Aylwin
Wright
Point Comfort
La Conception
Gray Rocks
Sheenboro
Nicabong
Waltham
Mont-Ste-Marie
Kazabazua
Lac-des-Plages
Mont-Tremblant
Fort William
Chichester
Davidson
Low
Bowman
Val-des-Bois
Chénéville
St-Jovite
Petawawa
Chapeau
Danford Lake
Denholm
Namur
Mont Blanc
St-Rémi-d'Amherst
Demers Centre
Fort-Coulonge
Venosta
Notre-Dame-de-la-Salette
Ripon
St-André-Avellin
Pembroke
Vinton
Otter Lake
Ski Vorlage
St-Pierre-de-Wakefield
Boileau
Desjardinsville
Thorney
Schwartz
Edelweiss Val-des-Monts
St-Sixte
Beachburg
Campbell's Bay
Lac-des-Loups
Montebello Calumet
Micksburg
Bryson
Charteris
Duclos
St-François-de-Masham
Papineau Manor N.H.S.
Cobden
Shawville
Portage-du-Fort
Wakefield
Plaisance
Granville
Renfrew
Killaloe
Reinke's Hill
Île-du-Grand-Calumet
Onslow Corners
Mayo
Papineauville
Fasset
Eganville
Golden L.
Quyon
Buckham's Bay
Gatineau
Hawkesbury
Braeside
Norway Bay
Bristol
Eardley
Chelsea
Buckingham
Rockland
Vankleek Hill
Arnprior
L. Clear
Cascades
Thurso
Angers
Alfred
Plantagenet
Bourget
Kanata
Aylmer
Hull
Vanier
Ottawa
Vars
St. Isidore
Ste-Justine-de-Newton
Nepean
Gloucester
Embrun
Alexandria
Black Donald Lake
Almonte
Russell
Maxville
Carleton Place
Richmond
Metcalfe
Monkland
ON 148
Lanark
Kars
Winchester
Avonmore
Martintown
Blacks Corners
Mulloys
Chesterville
Apple Hill
Perth
Smiths Falls
Kemptville
Williamsburg
Finch
St. Andrews
BON ÉCHO PROV. PARK
Merrickville
Spencerville
Morrisburg
Madrid
Norwood
Sharbot Lake
Long Sault
Cornwall
NY 94
Massena
ST. REGIS MOHAWK IND. RES.
Fort Covington

OTTAWA

Gatineau
Promenade de l'Outaouais
Île Kettle
CAN. FORCES BASE OTTAWA (NORTH)
Upper Duck I.
© MQST
GATINEAU PARK
Hull
Rockcliffe Park
National Aviation Museum
Gloucester
Rockcliffe
Rideau Hall
Vanier
NATL. RESEARCH COUNCIL LABORATORIES
Aylmer
Hull Train Station
Natl. Gallery of Canada
Parliament Hill
RCMP Hdqrs.
JetForm Park
Currency Museum
Mus. of Nature
Univ. of Ottawa
Ottawa Train Station
Billings Estate Museum
QUÉBEC ONTARIO
Natl. Library
Univ. of Québec à Hull
NATIONAL MUSEUM OF SCIENCE AND TECHNOLOGY
St. Paul Univ.
Observatory
Botanic Garden & Arboretum
DND
CENTRAL EXPERIMENTAL FARM
Rideau Canal and Locks
Carleton Univ.
Billings Estate Museum
Collingwood Shop Ctr.
Boy Scouts of Canada Museum
Ottawa
Nepean

0 0.5 1 mi
0 0.5 1 km

	BAIE-COMEAU	CHICOUTIMI	DRUMMONDVILLE	GASPÉ	MONT-LAURIER	MONTRÉAL	OTTAWA ON	QUÉBEC	RIMOUSKI	RIVIÈRE-DU-LOUP	ROBERVAL	ROUYN-NORANDA	ST-GEORGES	SEPT-ÎLES	SHERBROOKE	SOREL	TROIS-RIVIÈRES	VICTORIAVILLE
MONTRÉAL	663	461	116	898	230	—	194	250	535	426	448	616	325	887	143	87	146	164
QUÉBEC	400	211	151	668	439	250	444	—	305	'196	253	789	102	624	233	204	135	114
RIVIÈRE-DU-LOUP	230*	154*	328	472	656	426	620	196	109	—	249*	1042	274	454*	401	381	333	291
SHERBROOKE	633	444	82	873	373	143	337	233	510	401	417	759	148	857	—	142	158	97
TROIS-RIVIÈRES	535	346	68	804	376	146	340	135	447	333	296	762	214	759	158	82	—	65

DRIVING DISTANCES IN KILOMETERS   * DISTANCE INCLUDES FERRY TRAVEL

152 MARITIMES

DRIVING DISTANCES IN KILOMETERS
*DISTANCE INCLUDES FERRY TRAVEL

	BATHURST, NB	CAMPBELLTON, NB	CHARLOTTETOWN, PE	DIGBY, NS	EDMUNDSTON, NB	FREDERICTON, NB	GASPÉ, QC	HALIFAX, NS	LUNENBURG, NS	MIRAMICHI, NB	MONCTON, NB	NEW GLASGOW, NS	PORT HAWKESBURY, NS	RIMOUSKI, QC	RIVIÈRE-DU-LOUP, QC	SAINT JOHN, NB	ST. STEPHEN, NB	SYDNEY, NS	TRURO, NS	WOODSTOCK, NB	YARMOUTH, NS
CHARLOTTETOWN, PE	328	434		539	629	354	730	322	419	258	162	110*	224*	620	749	312	457	616			
FREDERICTON, NB	245	351	354	669	275		647	452	549	175	192	425	539	445	395	105	123	689	363	105	
HALIFAX, NS	452	558	322	217	727	452	854		97	382	260	151	265	744	847	410	515	415	89	555	294
SAINT JOHN, NB	350	456	312	82*	380	175	752	410	228*	280	150	383	497	550	500		105	647	321	208	176*
SYDNEY, NS	689	795	374*	632	964	689	1091	415	512	619	497	264	123	981	1084	647	752		326	792	709

DISTANCES IN CANADA SHOWN IN KILOMETERS

© MapQuest.com, Inc.

	BONAVISTA	CHAN.-PT. AUX BASQUES	DEER LAKE	GANDER	GRAND FALLS-WINDSOR	MARYSTOWN	ST. ANTHONY	ST. JOHN'S	STEPHENVILLE
	BISHOP'S FALLS	CORNER BROOK							
ARGENTIA	363	266	845	643	588	291	381	263	991	134	702
BISHOP'S FALLS	363		307	482	280	225	72	18	384	628	393	339
CHAN.-PT.AUX BASQUES	845	482		789		202	257	554	464	866	660	875	151
CORNER BROOK	643	280	587		202		55	352	262	664	458	673	59
ST. JOHN'S	134	393	296	875	673	618	321	411	293	1021		732

DRIVING DISTANCES IN KILOMETERS — ALL TOWNS ON THIS CHART ARE LOCATED IN NEWFOUNDLAND

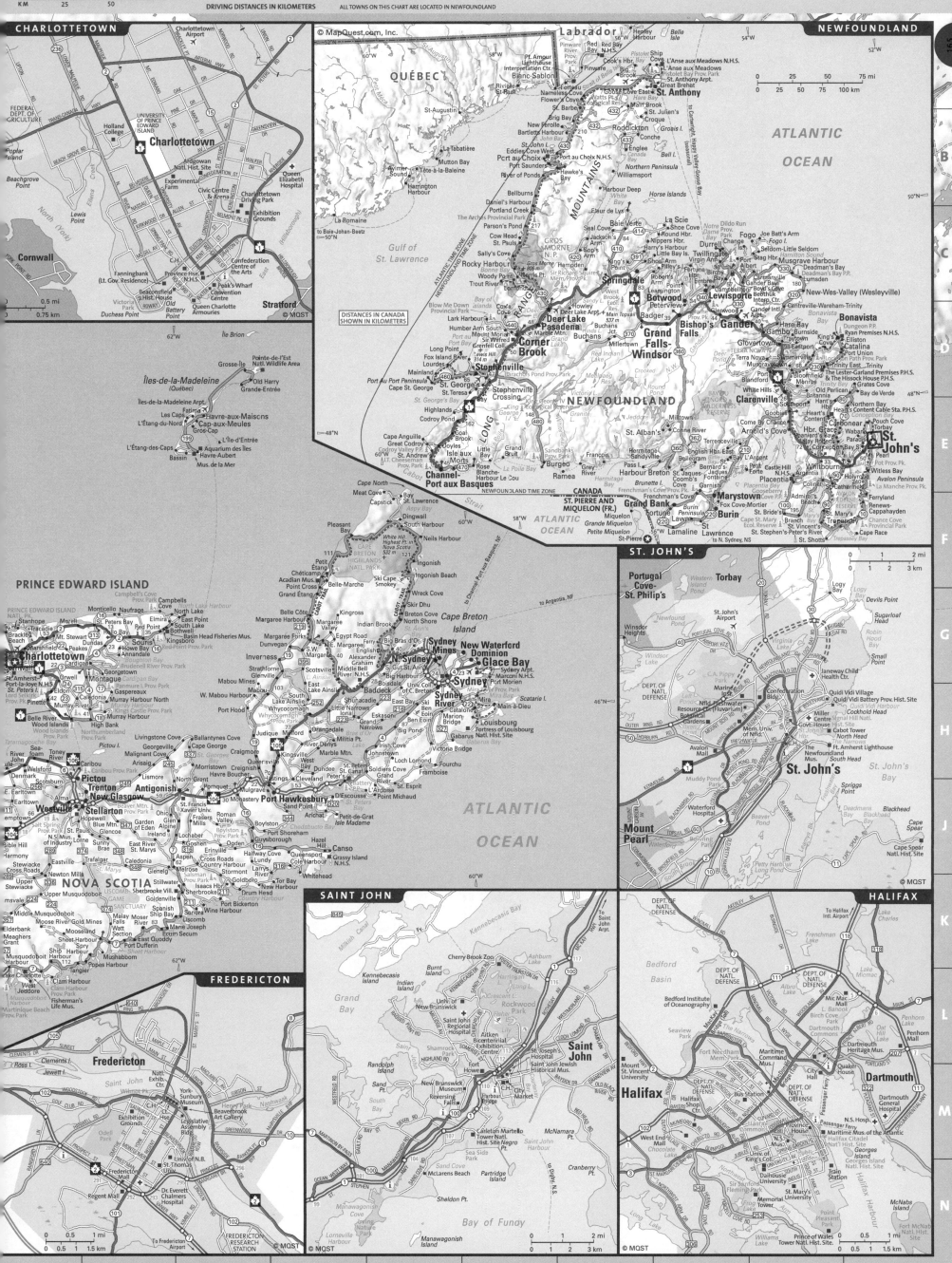

MI 75 150
KM 75 150

Insets:
MAZATLÁN
MEXICO CITY
ACAPULCO

States/Regions:
ARIZONA
NEW MEXICO
SONORA
CHIHUAHUA
SIERRA MADRE OCCIDENTAL
SIERRA MADRE ORIENTAL
BAJA CALIFORNIA
BAJA CALIFORNIA SUR
SINALOA
DURANGO
COAHUILA
ZACATECAS
NAYARIT
JALISCO
MICHOACÁN
COLIMA
UNITED STATES / MÉXICO
PACIFIC OCEAN

Major cities and towns:
San Diego, Tijuana, Mexicali, Calexico, Yuma, San Luis Río Colorado, Ensenada, El Sauzal, Tucson, Nogales, Las Cruces, El Paso, Ciudad Juárez, Midland, Hermosillo, Caborca, Cananea, Agua Prieta, Nuevo Casas Grandes, Chihuahua, Cuauhtémoc, Delicias, Ciudad Obregón, Guaymas, Empalme, Navojoa, Huatabampo, Los Mochis, Culiacán, Hidalgo del Parral, Gómez Palacio, Torreón, Durango, Fresnillo, Zacatecas, Aguascalientes, La Paz, Mazatlán, Tepic, Puerto Vallarta, Zapopan, Tlaquepaque, Guadalajara, León, Lagos de Moreno, San Francisco del Rincón, Ciudad Guzmán, Colima, Manzanillo, Tecomán, Apatzingán, Uruapan, Lázaro Cárdenas, Zihuatanejo

MAZATLÁN inset:
CERRITOS BEACH, SÁBALO BEACH, Plaza de Toros, Aquarium, City Museum, Mazatlán, Railroad Station, City Hall, Federal Palace, LA PIEDRA PENINSULA, Cresto Hill Lighthouse, El Castillo, PACIFIC OCEAN, Rafael Buelna International Airport

MEXICO CITY inset:
Nicolás Romero, Cuautitlán Izcalli, Tultitlán, Coacalco, Ciudad López Mateos, Fuentes del Valle, Buenavista, Ecatepec de Morelos, Santa Clara, Tlalnepantla, Tepexpan, Tezoyuca, Chiconcuac, San Salvador Atenco, Tulantongo, Texcoco, México, Naucalpan, Santiago Tepatlaxco, Cuajimalpa, Magdalena Chichicaspa, San Miguel Coatinchan, Santiago Cuautlalpan, Chimalhuacán, San Vicente Chicoloapan, Netzahualcóyotl, Los Reyes, Ixtapaluca, Ayotla, Xochimilco, Tláhuac, Chalco, San Mateo Huitzilzingo, Milpa Alta, Benito Juárez Intl. Airport, Olympic Stadium, Aztec Stadium, University City

ACAPULCO inset:
Reforma Agraria, Fine Arts Regional Center, Convention Center, Icacos Beach, La Quebrada Diving Gorge, La Paloma Beach, Bull Ring, Acapulco, Bahía de Acapulco, Puerto Marqués, Juan N. Álvarez International Airport, PACIFIC OCEAN

© MQST

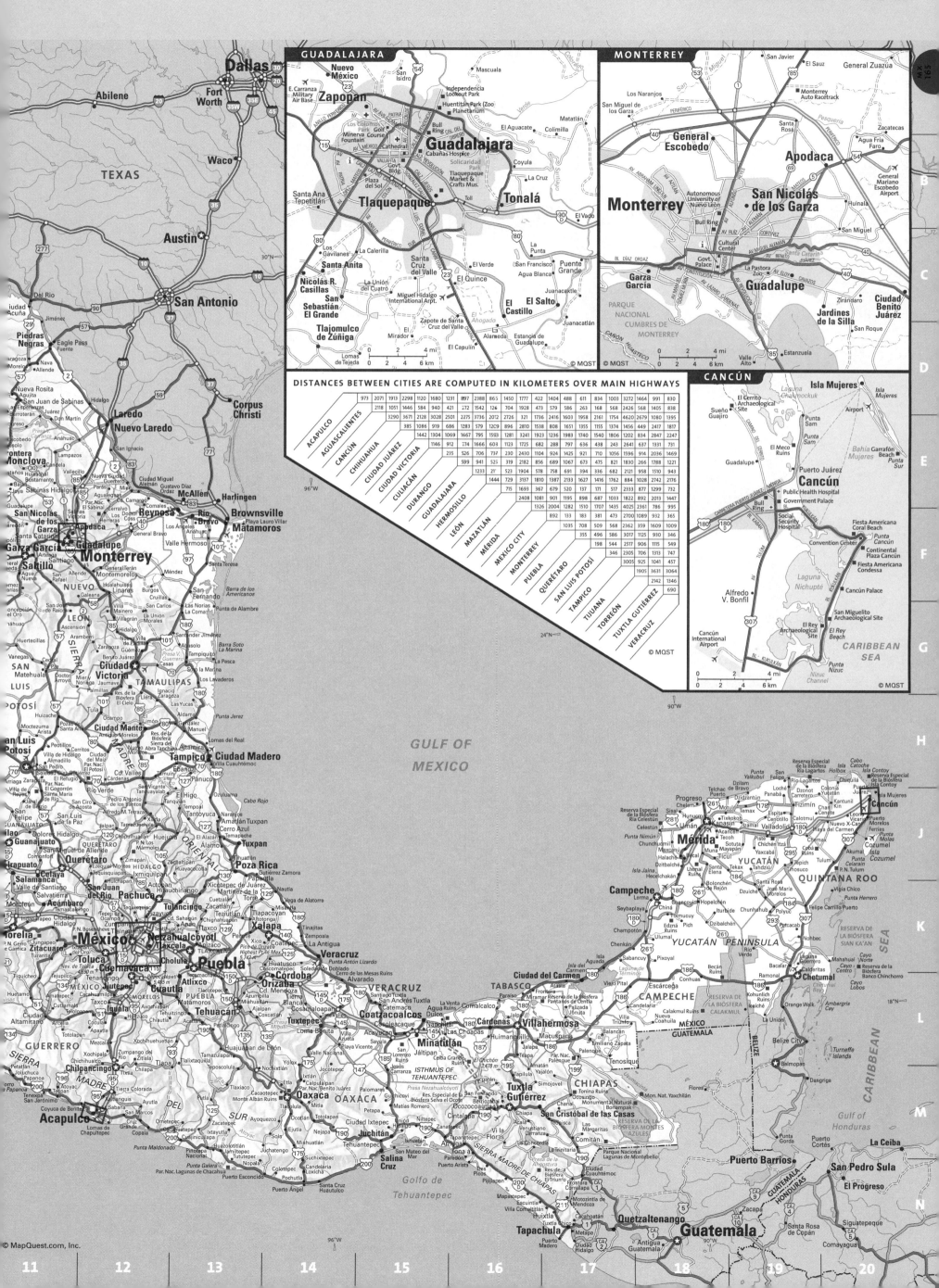

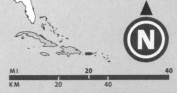

	AGUADILLA	ARECIBO	CAGUAS	CAYEY	FAJARDO	GUAYAMA	HUMACAO	MANATÍ	MAYAGÜEZ	PONCE	SAN JUAN	UTUADO
ARECIBO	32		59	70	80	87	74	17	48	52	48	20
CAGUAS	90	59		12	36	28	17	41	97	50	17	76
MAYAGÜEZ	16	48	97	85	129	84	114	64		46	96	48
PONCE	62	52	50	39	85	37	67	52	46		67	32
SAN JUAN	80	48	17	28	34	44	33	31	96	67		67

DRIVING DISTANCES IN MILES

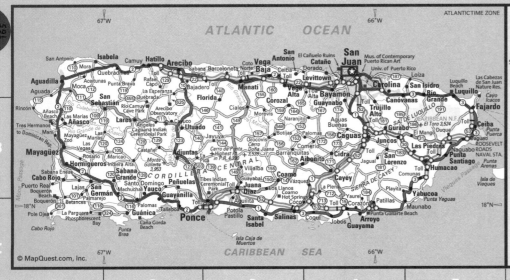

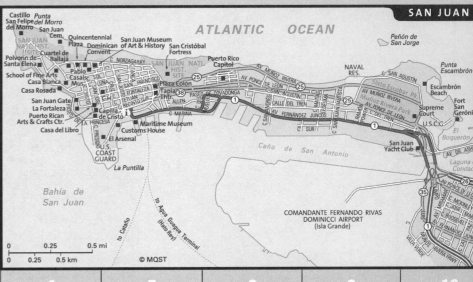

SAN JUAN

© MapQuest.com, Inc.

© MQST

Alabama–California

Note: Population figures are from the latest census or the most recent available estimates.

ALABAMA
PG. 22–23

25AA123

CAPITAL
Montgomery

NICKNAME
Heart of Dixie

POPULATION
4,351,999, rank 23

AREA
51,705 sq mi, rank 29

Counties

Cities and Towns

ALASKA
PG. 24

DBA 123

CAPITAL
Juneau

NICKNAME
Great Land

POPULATION
614,010, rank 48

AREA
591,004 sq mi, rank 1

Cities and Towns

ARIZONA
PG. 25–27

001·AAA

CAPITAL
Phoenix

NICKNAME
Grand Canyon State

POPULATION
4,668,631, rank 21

AREA
114,000 sq mi, rank 6

Counties

Cities and Towns
City indexed to pg. 25

ARKANSAS
PG. 28–29

941 ABA

CAPITAL
Little Rock

NICKNAME
Natural State

POPULATION
2,538,303, rank 33

AREA
53,187 sq mi, rank 27

Counties

Cities and Towns

CALIFORNIA
PG. 30–37

3MBC123

CAPITAL
Sacramento

NICKNAME
Golden State

POPULATION
32,666,550, rank 1

AREA
158,706 sq mi, rank 3

Counties

Cities and Towns
City indexed to pg. 34-35

GUNTERSVILLE LAKE, AL

TOKLAT RIVER, DENALI NATIONAL PARK, AK

HALF DOME AND NEVADA FALL, YOSEMITE NATIONAL PARK, CA

COLORADO
PG. 37–39

CAPITAL
Denver

NICKNAME
Centennial State

POPULATION
3,970,971, rank 24

AREA
104,091 sq mi, rank 8

Counties

Cities and Towns

CONNECTICUT
PG. 40–41

CAPITAL
Hartford

NICKNAME
Constitution State

POPULATION
3,274,069, rank 29

AREA
5,018 sq mi, rank 48

Counties

Cities and Towns
*City indexed to pg. 37

DELAWARE
PG. 42

CAPITAL
Dover

NICKNAME
First State

POPULATION
743,603, rank 45

AREA
2,044 sq mi, rank 49

Counties

Cities and Towns

DISTRICT OF COLUMBIA
PG. 136

CAPITAL

POPULATION
523,124

AREA
69 sq mi

Washington, 523'24

FLORIDA
PG. 43–46

CAPITAL
Tallahassee

NICKNAME
Sunshine State

POPULATION
14,915,980, rank 4

AREA
58,664 sq mi, rank 22

Counties

Cities and Towns
*City indexed to pg. 43

GEORGIA
PG. 47–49

CAPITAL
Atlanta

NICKNAME
Empire State of the South

POPULATION
7,642,207, rank 10

AREA
58,910 sq mi, rank 21

Cities and Towns
*City indexed to pg. 47

CLIFF PALACE, MESA VERDE NATIONAL PARK, CO

IDAHO
PG. 51

CAPITAL
Boise

NICKNAME
Gem State

POPULATION
1,228,684, rank 40

AREA
83,564 sq mi, rank 13

HAWAII
PG. 50

CAPITAL
Honolulu

NICKNAME
Aloha State

POPULATION
1,193,001, rank 41

AREA
6,471 sq mi, rank 47

ILLINOIS
PG. 52–55

CAPITAL
Springfield

NICKNAME
Land of Lincoln

POPULATION
12,045,326, rank 5

AREA
56,345 sq mi, rank 24

INDIANA
PG. 55–57

CAPITAL
Indianapolis

NICKNAME
Hoosier State

POPULATION
5,899,195, rank 14

AREA
36,185 sq mi, rank 38

IOWA
PG. 58–59

CAPITAL
Des Moines

NICKNAME
Hawkeye State

POPULATION
2,862,447, rank 30

AREA
56,275 sq mi, rank 25

KANSAS
PG. 60–61

CAPITAL
Topeka

NICKNAME
Sunflower State

POPULATION
2,629,067, rank 32

AREA
82,277 sq mi, rank 14

KENNEDY SPACE CENTER, FL

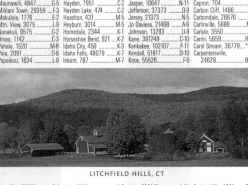

LITCHFIELD HILLS, CT

SUN VALLEY, ID

LOUISIANA
PG. 64–65

EPV 024

CAPITAL
Baton Rouge

NICKNAME
Pelican State

POPULATION
4,368,967, rank 22

AREA
47,751 sq mi, rank 31

Parishes

KENTUCKY
PG. 62–63

123 ABC

CAPITAL
Frankfort

NICKNAME
Bluegrass State

POPULATION
3,936,499, rank 25

AREA
40,409 sq mi, rank 37

Counties

Cities and Towns

MAINE
PG. 66–67

ABC-123

CAPITAL
Augusta

NICKNAME
Fine Tree State

POPULATION
1,244,250, rank 39

AREA
33,265 sq mi, rank 39

Counties

Cities and Towns

MARYLAND
PG. 68–70

ABC 123

CAPITAL
Annapolis

NICKNAME
Old Line State

POPULATION
5,134,808, rank 19

AREA
10,460 sq mi, rank 42

Counties

Cities and Towns
* City indexed to pg. 70
# Independent city
population not included
in county total

MAMMOTH CAVE NATIONAL PARK, KY

MASSACHUSETTS
PG. 71–73

123-ZBC

CAPITAL
Boston

NICKNAME
Bay State

POPULATION
6,147,132, rank 13

AREA
8,284 sq mi, rank 45

Counties

Cities and Towns
* City indexed to pg. 71

MICHIGAN
PG. 74–76

ABC 123

CAPITAL
Lansing

NICKNAME
Great Lakes State

POPULATION
9,817,242, rank 8

AREA
58,527 sq mi, rank 23

Counties

Cities and Towns
*City indexed to pg. 76

MINNESOTA
PG. 77–79

123 KBC
10,000 lakes

CAPITAL
St. Paul

NICKNAME
Gopher State

POPULATION
4,725,419, rank 20

AREA
84,402 sq mi, rank 12

Counties

Cities and Towns
*City indexed to pg. 77

MISSISSIPPI
PG. 80

ABC 123
COUNTY

CAPITAL
Jackson

NICKNAME
Magnolia State

POPULATION
2,752,092, rank 31

AREA
47,689 sq mi, rank 32

Counties

Cities and Towns

MISSOURI
PG. 81–83

123 ABC

CAPITAL
Jefferson City

NICKNAME
Show Me State

POPULATION
5,438,559, rank 16

AREA
69,697 sq mi, rank 19

Counties

Cities and Towns

OAK ALLEY PLANTATION, VACHERIE, LA

PEMAQUID POINT LIGHTHOUSE, ME

MONTANA
PG. 84–85

5P·1234A

CAPITAL
Helena

NICKNAME
Treasure State

POPULATION
880,453, rank 44

AREA
147,046 sq mi, rank 4

Counties

Cities and Towns
*City indexed to pg. 81
Independent city
population not included in county figures.

NEBRASKA
PG. 86–87

94·A12

CAPITAL
Lincoln

NICKNAME
Cornhusker State

POPULATION
1,662,719, rank 3

AREA
77,355 sq mi, rank

Counties

Cities and Towns

NEVADA
PG. 88

123•HBC

CAPITAL
Carson City

NICKNAME
Silver State

POPULATION
1,746,898, rank 36

AREA
110,561 sq mi, rank 7

Counties

Cities and Towns
Independent city
population not included
in county figures.

ASSATEAGUE ISLAND, MD

NEW HAMPSHIRE
PG. 89

123 456

CAPITAL
Concord

NICKNAME
Granite State

POPULATION
1,185,048, rank 42

AREA
9,279 sq mi, rank 44

Counties

Cities and Towns

NEW JERSEY
PG. 90–91

KZ •123C
Garden State

CAPITAL
Trenton

NICKNAME
Garden State

POPULATION
8,115,011, rank 9

AREA
7,787 sq mi, rank 46

Counties

NEW MEXICO
PG. 92–93

001•GHB
New Mexico USA

CAPITAL
Santa Fe

NICKNAME
Land of Enchantment

POPULATION
1,736,931, rank 37

AREA
121,593 sq mi, rank 5

Counties

Cities and Towns

NEW YORK
PG. 94–99

A12 3BC

CAPITAL
Albany

NICKNAME
Empire State

POPULATION
18,175,301, rank 3

AREA
49,108 sq mi, rank 30

Cities and Towns

GREAT HALL, GRAND PORTAGE NATIONAL MONUMENT, MN

NORTH CAROLINA
PG. 100–102

GZA-1234
NORTH CAROLINA

CAPITAL
Raleigh

NICKNAME
Tar Heel State

POPULATION
7,546,493, rank 11

AREA
52,669 sq mi, rank 28

Counties

Cities and Towns
City indexed to pg. 102

North Carolina

Cities and Towns

(extensive alphabetical place-name index listing cities and towns with population and grid references)

NORTH DAKOTA
PG. 103

DAA 123 · NORTH DAKOTA

CAPITAL
Bismarck

NICKNAME
Flickertail State

POPULATION
638,244, rank 47

AREA
70,703 sq mi, rank 17

Counties

Cities and Towns

OHIO
PG. 104–107

123 ABC · OHIO

CAPITAL
Columbus

NICKNAME
Buckeye State

POPULATION
11,209,493, rank 7

AREA
41,330 sq mi, rank 35

Counties

Cities and Towns

BIG BEND NATIONAL PARK, TX

OKLAHOMA
PG. 108–109

WLW 789 · OKLAHOMA

CAPITAL
Oklahoma City

NICKNAME
Sooner State

POPULATION
3,346,713, rank 27

AREA
69,956 sq mi, rank 18

Counties

Cities and Towns

OREGON
PG. 110–111

UBC 123 · Oregon

CAPITAL
Salem

NICKNAME
Beaver State

POPULATION
3,281,974, rank 28

AREA
97,073 sq mi, rank 10

Counties

Cities and Towns

PENNSYLVANIA
PG. 112–116

BAA·1234 · KEYSTONE STATE · PENNSYLVANIA

CAPITAL
Harrisburg

NICKNAME
Keystone State

POPULATION
12,001,451, rank 6

AREA
45,308 sq mi, rank 33

Counties

Cities and Towns
* City indexed by inset

WHEAT FIELD, NE

SKYLINE DRIVE, SHENANDOAH NATIONAL PARK, VA

RHODE ISLAND
PG. 117

★ Rhode Island ★
AA-123
— Ocean State — 10-11

CAPITAL
Providence

NICKNAME
Ocean State

POPULATION
988,480, rank 43

AREA
1,212 sq mi, rank 50

Counties

Cities and Towns

SOUTH DAKOTA
PG. 119

South Dakota
24A1234

CAPITAL
Pierre

NICKNAME
Mount Rushmore State

POPULATION
738,171, rank 46

AREA
77,116 sq mi, rank 16

Counties

Cities and Towns

SOUTH CAROLINA
PG. 118

Smiling Faces, Beautiful Places
123 ABC

CAPITAL
Columbia

NICKNAME
Palmetto State

POPULATION
3,835,962, rank 26

AREA
31,113 sq mi, rank 40

Counties

Cities and Towns

TENNESSEE
PG. 120–121

Tennessee
123 ABC

CAPITAL
Nashville

NICKNAME
Volunteer State

POPULATION
5,430,621, rank 17

AREA
42,144 sq mi, rank 34

Counties

Cities and Towns
* City indexed to pg. 126

SAN JUAN ISLANDS, WA

TEXAS
PG. 122–126

TEXAS
B01·BBB
— The Lone Star State —

CAPITAL
Austin

NICKNAME
Lone Star State

POPULATION
19,759,614, rank 2

AREA
266,807 sq mi, rank 2

Counties

Cities and Towns